T5-ANV-404

INSTITUTE OF NEW YORK AREA STUDIES
THE CITY COLLEGE OF NEW YORK
MONOGRAPH NO. 4

Nassau County: Its Governments and Their Expenditure and Revenue Patterns

SAMUEL F. THOMAS

Assistant Dean
Bernard M. Baruch School of
Business and Public Administration
The City College of New York

CITY COLLEGE PRESS
NEW YORK
1960

LIBRARY OF CONGRESS CATALOG CARD NUMBER: 60:15981
MANUFACTURED IN THE UNITED STATES OF AMERICA

DISTRIBUTED BY
ASSOCIATED COLLEGE PRESSES
32 WASHINGTON PLACE, NEW YORK CITY 3

FOREWORD

In 1954, the Rockefeller Foundation made a research grant to The City College for the purpose of developing materials and courses of study at the graduate level on the New York metropolitan area as a focus of American urban civilization. A companion grant from the Lucius N. Littauer Foundation made possible the establishment of a program of graduate instruction in which the products of research might be utilized as resource materials in seminar and classroom.

The administration of the project was lodged in a faculty group known as the New York Area Research Council which evolved a prospectus of research and a course of study leading to the M.A. degree. Both the research project and the course of study were centered in the general theme of "The New York Metropolitan Area as a Viable or an Adequately Effective Functioning Community." The individual investigations and the individual courses were designed to help define the distinctive character of the New York metropolitan community, to note its development, how it operates, what its shortcomings are, and the extent to which it has been successful in producing a good life for its citizens.

The pilot phase of this project came to an end in 1957, but the research as well as the graduate program of instruction have been continued. The latter is part of the Graduate Division of the College of Liberal Arts and Science, and the research work has been reorganized and consolidated in an Institute of New York Area Studies, inaugurated with the aid of a modest grant from the Wollman Foundation.

The research effort has yielded varied results. Faculty strength in this field of specialization has been identified, and experimentation with a variety of subjects has indicated the areas in which the best progress might be achieved. A satisfactory procedure has been evolved whereby group guidance has served to stimulate and clarify individual investigation. The research has been done by specialists employing the methodology of their respective disciplines, but the Research Council has met periodically and considered general objectives, the goals and interrelationships of the research segments, their relevance to the central theme, and the techniques employed in each study.

The amount of research done under this project has been considerable. Of more than twenty studies initiated, eight have been published, seven are in manuscript, and the remainder are in progress.

This volume is the work of Professor Samuel F. Thomas, Assistant Dean in the Bernard M. Baruch School of Business and Public Administration of The City College. As this work developed, Professor Thomas reported to the Research Council, of which he is a member, and his colleagues offered comments and suggestions. The book was also read in manuscript by a number of the members of the Research Council who found it a significant contribution and recommended its publication. However, each author associated with the project makes the final decisions in matters of content, methodology, and point of view of his work, and each author assumes the responsibility connected with a work of scholarship.

OSCAR I. JANOWSKY, *Director*
Institute of New York Area Studies
The City College of New York
April, 1960

PREFACE

This study was undertaken as part of the New York area research program, sponsored by the Rockefeller Foundation, at The City College of New York. The premise underlying the study is that we do not have a clear picture of the existing patterns of expenditures and income of governmental units in the metropolitan area. The total revenue of the area is expended in terms of priority needs determined politically by tradition, pressures, economic resources, political power, and constitutional and legislative provisions rather than by rational judgments in the light of expert advice as to what amounts of money, derived from which sources, should be spent to serve best the interests of the total metropolitan area.

The following pages attempt to shed some light on the fiscal problems of metropolitan New York by reviewing the governmental structure, expenditure and revenue patterns of the fastest growing county in the most populous metropolitan area in America: Nassau. In many ways this study of Nassau represents one of the more comprehensive pictures of how Nassau is governed and how much money is spent in the process.

This treatment of the subject includes an inventory of the governmental units in Nassau County; an inventory of the agencies of the units of government involved in fiscal operations; considerations of the expenditures and revenues of these units in 1945 and 1954; their 1956 budgets and observations on the adequacy of the existing governmental structure.

The author considers this monograph as a necessary first step to the understanding of the governmental problems facing Nassau, and the entire New York area. The absence of such a body of data on this particular county shaped the predominantly descriptive nature of this presentation. Once there is a comparable body of data on the rest of the New York area's political jurisdictions, then an analytical consideration of the fiscal and governmental problems facing the entire metropolitan area will be possible. Indeed, a comparison of Nassau's experience with those of other governmental units in the New York area will put its problems in a more meaningful perspective.

A second step in the plan to obtain comparable data on the other parts of the New York area has been completed. A companion manuscript on New York City's political jurisdiction and their expenditure and revenue patterns has been presented by the author to the Research Council of the Institute of New York Area Studies. A section of this report contains a comparative treatment of the fiscal problems of the urban center and the largest unit of the suburban fringe. Further studies of other segments of the metropolitan fringe will permit the identification of the similarities and differences of their problems and those confronting Nassau County.

The data in this report leads to the conclusion that the governmental structure of Nassau is inadequate for the task of serving the needs of an urban area. There is a need for a thorough reorganization of the county's existing pattern of government. To what degree is this true of the rest of the New York area? The answer must await further reseach efforts.

The author hopes that this study of Nassau County will serve to facilitate the understanding of the problems involved in the total complex of the metropolitan area as well as those of its fastest growing unit. A comparative study of the expenditure and revenue patterns and governmental structure of Westchester County is an appropriate next step.

Research work of the type represented in the preparation of this report places one in heavy debt to the people who so willingly shared of their knowledge to facilitate the completion of the assignment.

The writer is particularly indebted to Dr. Oscar Janowsky and the New York Area Program for making this study possible. The author found all the county, town, village, and school district officers and employees from whom he sought aid most helpful in supplying data, often at a great sacrifice of their time and energy.

PREFACE

The officers of the State Department of Education and the State Comptroller's office proved to be an invaluable and co-operative source of pertinent material. Dean Emanuel Saxe deserves a special word of thanks for his encouragement and support.

Publication of this study was made feasible by a Lucius N. Littauer Foundation Grant. The author is pleased to acknowledge this assistance.

S. F. THOMAS
December, 1958

CONTENTS

TABLES

TABLES

TABLES

CHARTS AND MAPS

Nassau County: Its Governments and Their Expenditure and Revenue Patterns

Introduction

DYNAMIC NASSAU

Nassau County, one of the fastest growing areas in the United States, is located on Long Island. Bounded on the west by New York City, on the east by Suffolk County, on the north by Long Island Sound, and on the south by the Atlantic Ocean, Nassau is a dynamic force in the economic, political, and social life of the New York metropolitan area.[1] Covering an area just under three hundred square miles, the county is one of the smallest in New York State.[2] In terms of population, it is challenging Erie County[3] for the title of most heavily populated county in the state outside of New York City.

The population of Nassau County is estimated at more than one million.[4] The federal census figures since 1900 reflect an extraordinary growth.

TABLE 1

Federal Census Figures

Year	Census
1900	55,448
1910	83,930
1920	126,120
1930	303,053
1940	406,748
1950	672,765

1 The New York metropolitan area consists of Fairfield County in Connecticut; Bergen, Essex, Hudson, Middlesex, Monmouth, Morris, Passaic, Somerset, and Union counties in New Jersey; Dutchess, Nassau, Orange, Putnam, Rockland, Suffolk, Westchester, and the five counties of New York City in New York State.

2 Three of the other fifty-seven counties in New York State, outside of New York City, are smaller in land area. The five counties that comprise New York City (Bronx, Kings, New York, Queens, and Richmond) cover a total land area of 315 square miles.

3 1950 census figures placed Nassau's population at 672,765 and Erie's at 899,238.

4 The estimate (1955) of the Long Island Lighting Company was 1,033,000.

The estimate of 1,033,000 residents as of January 1955 represents an increase of about 53 per cent over the 1950 census figures and seems to indicate that the rate of growth between 1950–1960 may well exceed that of the period from 1940 to 1950, when Nassau was the fastest growing urban county in the country. One population prognosis for this area is that Nassau County will have 1,592,000 residents in 1960.[5]

One cannot overlook the significance of these population trends with their obvious impact on the demands, both present and future, for more and more governmental services; nor can one ignore the economic, political, and social adjustments involved in such a rapid urbanization of a county governmentally structured to meet the needs of a quasi-rural and suburban community.

Closely paralleling this surging population growth and presenting an equal challenge to Nassau's governmental hierarchy are such problems as the increasing industrialization of the county; the large number of automobiles owned by county residents;[6] the never-ending construction of thousands of new homes; and the development of large suburban shopping centers. The difficulty is to provide efficient governmental services to cope with these changes —a problem the solution of which may well lie beyond the power, authority, and competence of the existing pattern of governmental jurisdictions in Nassau County.

THE NATURE OF GOVERNMENT IN NASSAU

Government in Nassau reflects the modification of a pattern of local government that can be traced back to the seventeenth century. An expert in New York State government recently observed[7]

[5] James W. Carpenter, "Population Prognosis," a paper presented at a planning forum held at Hofstra College, September 9, 1955. Mr. Carpenter stated that the Regional Plan Association estimates Nassau's 1960 population at 1,250,000. He also identified some interesting characteristics of the county's population. "Nassau people average 31.3 years of age, have 3.51 persons per family, have completed 12.1 school years (state average: 33.7 years, 3.27 persons per family, 9.6 school years completed). The county leads all others in our state in youthfulness and amount of schooling." This paper has been reproduced in a bulletin on the forum entitled "The Problems of Growth in Nassau and Western Suffolk."

[6] Estimated at over 400,000 or one car per family.

[7] Lynton K. Caldwell, *The Government and Administration of New York* (New York: Thomas Y. Crowell Company, 1954), p. 123.

that "local government in New York . . . presents not only a diversity required by contemporary conditions, but a complexity resulting from gradual and often uneven modification of traditional forms and practices." He further commented that "traditional practices only slightly changed over the years coexist with important innovations no older than the last session of the state legislature."[8] Nassau's governmental jurisdictions prove the truth of this generalization.

While many of Nassau County's governmental jurisdictions have their roots deep in colonial America, Nassau as a county has a comparatively brief history. It is interesting to note that the emergence of Nassau as a county is directly related to the consolidation in 1898 of the five counties that now constitute New York City. Prior to 1899 that part of Long Island now known as Nassau was part of Queens County. In that year the three eastern towns of Queens County—Hempstead, North Hempstead, and Oyster Bay—decided not to become part of the consolidated City of New York, declining to follow the other towns of Queens. The county of Nassau was thus born with a population in the vicinity of fifty thousand. Since then, time and circumstance have wrought considerable change in the number of municipal subdivisions providing governmental services; the kind and scope of the functions carried on by these units and the organization of each unit adequately to perform its assigned role in the total complex.

Local governmental services in Nassau County are provided by the following jurisdictions[9] or units of government:

1. The county
2. Towns
3. Cities
4. Villages
5. School Districts
6. Special Districts

These types of governmental jurisdiction are not unique or restricted to Nassau County, for they represent the basic types of

[8] *Ibid.*, p. 123.

[9] The federal, state, and specialized governmental jurisdictions not providing services solely in the county or not having the basic characteristics of unit local government are excluded from this tabulation.

local jurisdiction found throughout the state of New York. Before making a careful inventory of the governmental structure of each of these various types of jurisdiction in the county, it may be worthwhile to consider briefly the growth in the number of governmental subdivisions serving Nassau's residents, as well as the total number now in existence.

Like everything else in the county, the smaller units of government have evidenced a marked ability to multiply. The figures in the following table show the steady increase in the number of such units since 1920.

TABLE 2

Number of Villages, School Districts, and Other Special Districts in Nassau County

1920–1955	Villages	Special Districts [1]	School Districts	Total
1920 [2]	19	87	65	171
1925 [2]	28	125	66	219
1930 [2]	46	164	67	277
1933 [2]	63	173	65	301
1945 [3]	63	199	60	322
1955 [4]	63	268	62	393

[1] As of December 31 of each year, except 1955, which is as of August 1955.

[2] Figures taken from **The Government of Nassau County,** a report by the Municipal Consultant Service of the National Municipal League, Mineola, 1954, p. 4.

[3] Tabulation made from figures taken from the **Five Year Cumulative Report of the County of Nassau, New York and all Municipal Subdivisions,** compiled by the County Comptroller, 1945.

[4] Tabulation made from figures taken from the Report on Assessed Valuation, **Department of Assessment, County of Nassau,** August 1955 (mimeo), 21 pages.

The total number of municipal subdivisions in Nassau County today is approximately four hundred. This total includes:

1 County
2 Cities
63 Incorporated Villages
3 Towns
268 Special districts [10]
62 School districts

The pattern of growth in numbers of special districts and the

[10] See page 36. This figures does not reflect changes in the number of special districts since 1955.

standstill in the development of villages since 1933 is a characteristic of local government throughout New York State. There has not been a single incorporation of a city in Nassau since 1922 or of a village since 1932. In the entire state of New York, just two villages and two cities have been incorporated since 1940.[11]

This is extremely interesting because the population movement in Nassau County and in the entire state has been in the direction of "rural non-farm areas, the suburban residential and economic centers which would formerly have been organized into villages and cities."[12] Mr. J. Raymond McGovern advances the premise that:

> This decline in incorporation can be shown to be the outgrowth, at least in part, of the enactment of the new Town Law in 1933, becoming effective January 1, 1934. This new law gave broader powers to town governments to provide services formerly obtainable only through incorporation. By the establishment of special districts, towns may now provide fire protection, water, sewer, light and other services to those areas of the town in which such services are especially needed.[13]

The matter of taxation may well be significant in this avoidance of incorporation and wide acceptance of the special district approach. The use of special districts amounts to the earmarking of funds for particular services. The resident thus sees himself as paying directly for those services which he must have and which benefit him directly. Incorporation as a village not only operates on principles opposed to the earmarking of funds and the tracing of specific taxes to specific services rendered but leaves the resident with possibility of both village and town taxes on his property.

Moreover, this tendency toward what one authority calls governmental fragmentation of the fringe area of the metropolitan region is a characteristic of most metropolitan areas in the country today.[14]

In 1934, the Board of Supervisors of Nassau County were ad-

[11] J. R. McGovern, "Control and Supervision of Cities and Villages by the State," *Brooklyn Law Review,* April 1954.

[12] *Ibid.,* p. 161.

[13] *Ibid.,* p. 163.

[14] Charles Adrian, *Governing Urban America* (New York: McGraw-Hill, 1955), p. 42.

vised that the 301 villages and districts in the county was an excessive number and that "everything which reasonably can be done should be done to regulate the formation of new villages and districts and to reduce as far as possible the number now existing."[15] Twenty years later and with nearly a hundred additional special districts, the term "excessive" should be amended to read "far too excessive." Furthermore, the arguments advanced then against the proliferation of governmental jurisdictions are truer than ever.

The following section presents a more detailed consideration of each of the various types of local government operating in Nassau County, and their respective organizations for effective fiscal management of their affairs.

[15] Municipal Consultant Service of the National Municipal League, *The Government of Nassau County,* a report to the Board of Supervisors of Nassau County (Mineola, 1934), p. 4.

Part I

Nassau's Governments and Their Administration

Many thousands of residents of the central core of the New York metropolitan area, with its highly centralized government, who have migrated to suburban Nassau are for the most part either confused by or at best inexperienced with local government based on what one might call the "levels theory." Such a theory calls for the provision of particular services of local government by relatively autonomous municipal subdivisions operating at one of several levels with varying degrees of authority and responsibility. In time the recently established resident should be increasingly aware of some of the practical manifestations of this government by level or layer. He might soon realize, for example, that "the real burden of the Nassau County taxpayer is not Nassau County. Nor is it his town, or his village, or his school district, or any one of a number of other districts which may serve him. It is rather the combined weight of all the layers of government at once." [1]

Let us examine the way in which this stratification of home rule in Nassau County operates in terms of governmental administration, with emphasis on organization for financial management, at each of the following levels:

The County
The Towns and Special Districts
The Cities and Villages
The School Districts

[1] Municipal Consultant Service of the National Municipal League, *op. cit.*, p. 15. The taxpayer's understanding of the usual elements that constitute his total tax burden may be slight, if any, if he does as many new home owners in Nassau seem to be doing, i.e., paying their taxes to the bank with their monthly mortgage payments.

A. THE COUNTY

The county of Nassau is one of the sixty-two counties that constitute the total area of the state of New York. Barring the five counties that comprise New York City, Nassau, Westchester, and Monroe counties are usually identified as the only counties in the state that have made any real progress in the last twenty years in the reorganization of their county governments to meet the needs of the changing times. Nassau and Westchester played pioneer roles in the thirties in introducing what amounted to pilot projects in the creation of effective executive leadership, at the county level. They did this by establishing a County Executive to replace the old Board of Supervisors system that had led to a dispersion of responsibility.

In January 1938, Nassau County put into effect the first county charter in the state of New York, the main provisions of which have remained basically unchanged to this day.

Nassau County is a political subdivision of the state of New York. It is an arm of the government of the state as well as a unit of local government making and enforcing its own laws. As is true of all units of local government in the state, the county of Nassau functions as a political subdivision within the framework of the pertinent provisions of the state constitution, state legislative enactments, administrative regulations, and court decisions. The constitution, among other things, requires the legislature to "provide by law for the organization and government of counties";[2] limits the amount to be raised by real estate taxes for county purposes;[3] and places a limit of 10 per cent of the average full valuation of taxable real estate as the ceiling on county indebtedness.[4] Evidence of state supervision is found in such areas as civil service, and health and welfare. As a unit of local government Nassau functions under a charter adopted under the home rule provisions of the state constitution permitting counties to choose their form of government.

[2] *Constitution of New York State,* Art. IX, Sec. 1b.
[3] *Ibid.,* Art. VII, Sec. 10a.
[4] *Ibid.,* Art. VII, Sec. 4a.

The Organization of the County Government

The charter identifies the Board of Supervisors as the governing body of the county. It is both an administrative and a legislative body. It consists of the following officials:

1. The county executive, who is elected county-wide for a three year term.
2. Two supervisors of the town of Hempstead, who are elected for two years by the residents of the town of Hempstead.
3. One supervisor of the town of North Hempstead who is elected for two years by the residents of the town of North Hempstead.
4. One supervisor of the town of Oyster Bay who is elected for two years by the residents of the town of Oyster Bay.
5. One supervisor from the city of Glen Cove who is elected for two years by the residents of the city.
6. One supervisor from the city of Long Beach who is elected for four years by the residents of the city.

The county executive receives a salary of $25,000 a year. The other members of the Board of Supervisors are paid in part by the county for board duties and in part by the jurisdiction they represent on the board. The presiding supervisor of Hempstead, for example, receives $7,500 from the county and $10,000 from the town of Hempstead.

Voting on the Board

The county charter provides that:

> The supervisor or supervisors of each town and city, except as otherwise provided in this article, be entitled to cast at meetings of the board of supervisors, a number of votes equal to the quotient in whole numbers obtained by dividing the number of inhabitants, excluding aliens, as determined by the latest federal census or state census, whichever is the later, of the town or city from which they have been elected, by ten thousand; provided that when there is more than one supervisor from any town or city, the quotient so obtained shall be divided equally among the supervisors from such town or city, and further *provided that no*

supervisor shall have less than one vote, nor shall the supervisor or supervisors of any town or city be entitled to cast more than fifty per centum of the total vote of said board.[5]

The present apportionment of votes on the board, outlined below, seems to be in conflict with some of the provisions of the above sections of the law; in that Hempstead has 18 out of the 30 votes. This is clearly more than fifty per cent of the total.

Hempstead	18	9 presiding supervisor 9 supervisor
North Hempstead	7	
Oyster Bay	3	
Glen Cove	1	
Long Beach	1	
Total	30	

The county executive acts as the presiding officer of the Board of Supervisors and can vote only in case of a tie.

It should be noted that the only legislative body of the county government includes in its membership of seven people[6] six who are required to divide their efforts between their administrative and their legislative duties. They are not elected directly to membership on this board but serve as a result of having been elected to another post. The county executive heads the executive branch of the county; the town supervisors are responsible for the management of town affairs, and the mayor of Glen Cove has a considerable administrative load. This administrative work must certainly not only take much of their time but by definition staffs the Board of Supervisors with members whose interest is most likely to be heavily centered around the needs of their special limited governmental jurisdiction. The only member of the board who is elected county-wide has no vote, except in the rare case of a tie.

As the governing body of the county, the board creates, organizes, and abolishes departments, bureaus, and office positions

[5] *County Government Law of Nassau County,* Art. I, Sec. 104, 2. [Italics not in original.]

[6] City of Long Beach has a representative on the county board who does not hold an administrative post.

other than those specifically identified in the charter. It also sets the compensation of officers and employees; enacts legislation; makes appropriations; levies taxes, and incurs indebtedness. All action of the board is by ordinance or resolution on the basis of a majority vote. An ordinance requires the approval of the county executive. If not returned to the board in ten days, it is deemed approved. The board can override the executive's veto with a two-thirds vote.[7]

The County Executive

The charter charges the county executive with the preparation of and presentation to the board of the annual budget and an annual report on the financial and other transactions of the county. The county executive, as the administrative head of the county government, supervises the administration of all departments of the county government. He appoints, with board approval, the head of every county department and office and members of county boards and commissions. "He may at any time remove any person so appointed; provided that in the case of members of boards and commissions appointed for definite terms"[8] notice and a hearing are provided. The county executive appoints without confirmation by the Board of Supervisors the employees of his own office. Today the county executive office personnel includes the following: two deputy county executives and a small secretarial and clerical staff.

The Nassau County administrative code provides that the county executive "subject to confirmation by the board of supervisors, shall have the power to appoint, from time to time, a commission of taxpayers of Nassau County, not exceeding seventeen in number, who shall serve without compensation."[9] Such a commission may:

1. Examine the different laws of the state applicable to the government of the county, towns and other municipalities and political subdivisions

7 *County Government Law of Nassau County,* Art. I, Sec. 107.
8 *Ibid.,* Art. II, Sec. 203.
9 *Nassau County Administrative Code,* Chap. I, Title B, Sec. 1-7.0 (a).

in such county, and determine the advisability of changing the forms or methods of government of such county, towns or other political subdivisions.

2. Examine the form of government of other counties or cities within or without the State of New York, and the method used in the administrative, judicial, economic and other branches of such municipalities; for the purpose of recommending an improvement in the government of such county and its political subdivisions and from such examinations and investigations to determine what form of government is best suited to meet the needs of the residents of Nassau County.[10]

The significance of this will become more apparent as the reader reviews the existing pattern of local government detailed in the pages that follow.

Additional components in the organization of the county government and their relationship to the county executive and the Board of Supervisors are clearly depicted on the chart on page 13. It should be noted that while the number of elected county officials is reasonably small in number and reflects limited acceptance of the principle of the short ballot, the total number of governmental officials elected by the residents of the county to fill local governmental posts is considerable.

The purpose of this survey is to identify briefly the specific subdivisions of the governments concerned; detailed treatment is reserved for those agencies involved in the management of local fiscal affairs. Part II, dealing with expenditure and revenue patterns, will give the reader a rather comprehensive picture of what each level of government does and how these services are paid for.

We now turn our attention to the problem of who handles Nassau County's financial operations.

County Fiscal Administration

The management of Nassau County's fiscal affairs involves many officials and covers a variety of activities. The elements included under the heading County Fiscal Administration are considered in the following order: budgeting, revenue administration, treas-

[10] *Ibid.*

NASSAU COUNTY GOVERNMENTAL CHART

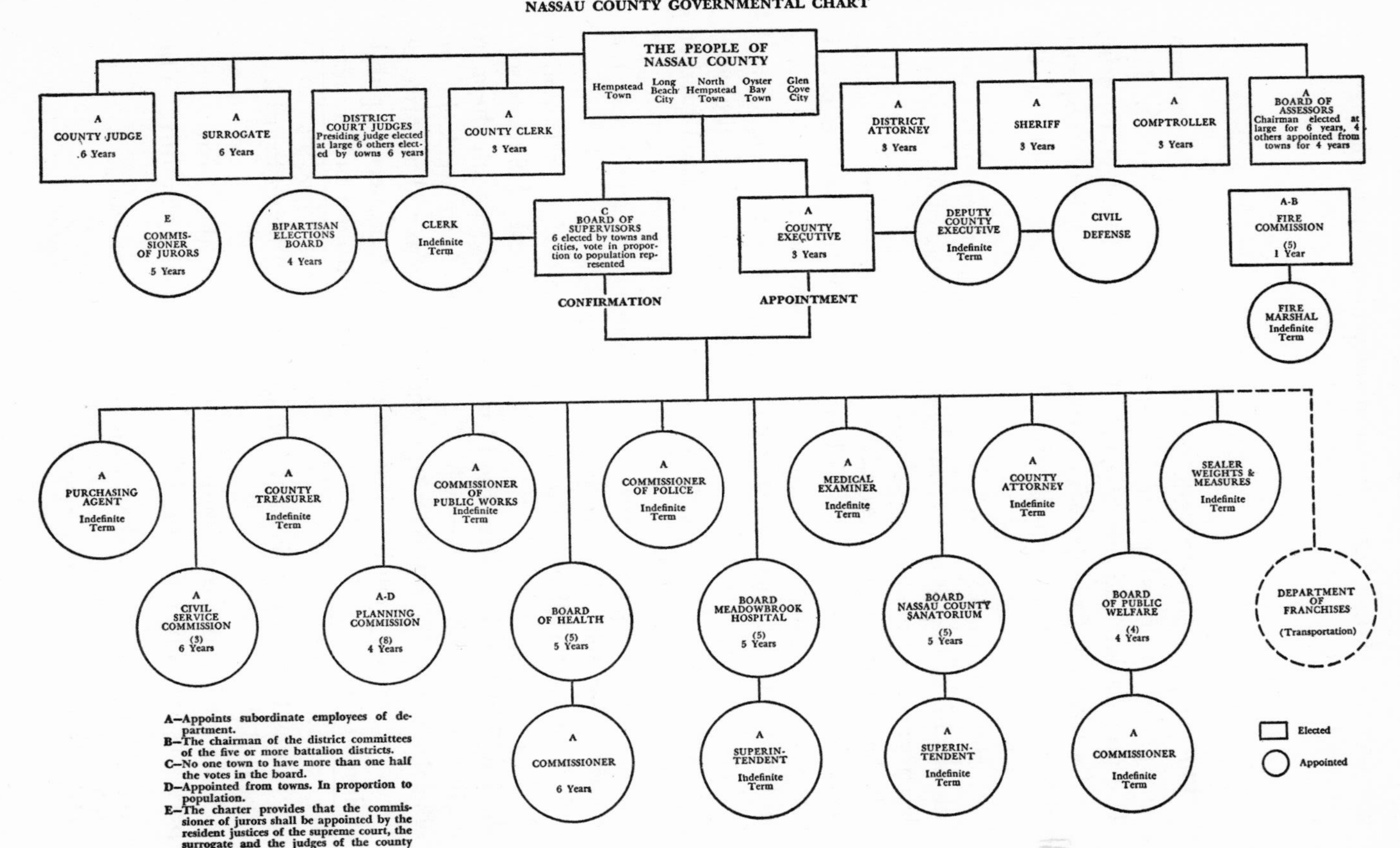

A—Appoints subordinate employees of department.
B—The chairman of the district committees of the five or more battalion districts.
C—No one town to have more than one half the votes in the board.
D—Appointed from towns. In proportion to population.
E—The charter provides that the commissioner of jurors shall be appointed by the resident justices of the supreme court, the surrogate and the judges of the county courts.

SOURCE: Nassau County, *Your County Nassau*, 1955.

ury management, accounting, auditing, financial reporting, and purchasing.

Budgeting

The county charter[11] deals specifically with the scope, preparation, presentation, adoption, and execution of the county budget. The preparation and presentation of the annual budget, covering the fiscal period from January through December, is the responsibility of the county executive. The budget process adheres to the following calendar:

1. Not later than September 15 each department or agency head submits his estimates of revenue and expenditure of his respective department to the county executive.

2. Not later than the second Monday in November, the county executive presents his proposed budget of revenue and expenditure for the ensuing fiscal year for the county, accompanied by a budget message explaining the main features of the budget and including a summary of it. The executive must submit at the same time a draft of an ordinance which need not be itemized further than by departments and by kind of expenditures [12] referring to the proposed budget and making provision for the conduct of the county government for the next fiscal year.

3. The matter of a public hearing on the budget is provided for in the charter in this language: "The Board of Supervisors shall within ten days after the filing of the budget with them in each year, publish at least twice, at intervals of one week, in the official newspapers, a copy of the budget message and a notice of the time, not less than five days after the date of the second publication, at which the board of supervisors will hold a public hearing on the county budget."[13] The law calls for the hearings to be adjourned from day to day until all interested in being heard have appeared.

4. Following the termination of the hearing, the Board of Supervisors may strike out or reduce any item of expenditure. The

[11] *County Government Law of Nassau County,* Art. III, Secs. 301–308.
[12] See page 73 for consideration of some aspects of 1956 budget.
[13] *County Government Law of Nassau County,* Art. III, Sec. 304.

insertion of any new item or an increase in an item of appropriation by the board requires it to publish a notice of the change and set a time for a public hearing. After the hearing "the Board of Supervisors may insert the additional item or items and make the increase or increases to the amount in each case indicated by the published notice or to a lesser amount; provided that the county executive may veto any such addition or increase and that no such addition or increase shall be passed over his veto by less than a two-thirds vote of the voting strength of the board."[14]

5. Not later than the third Monday in December the Board of Supervisors is required to have adopted the budget, passed the appropriation ordinance to implement it, and levied taxes for the ensuing year, including state, county, town, and special district taxes and assessments. The tax levies for the town and special districts must be approved by the board on the recommendation of town boards in the first case and the respective district commissioners in the latter.

The budget process does not terminate with the legislative enactment of the appropriation ordinance. The administrative control of expenditures is essential to effective management. This is accomplished at the county level through charter-required procedures involving departmental work programs and quarterly allotments that specify how much may be spent, for what, and when during the year. Additional controls over expenditure are provided in the form of restrictions on transfers of appropriations between departments and within departments. Such transfers require Board of Supervisors' approval as well as the county executive's recommendation; "supplemental appropriations from any moneys not otherwise appropriated may be made at any time upon recommendation of the county executive by a two-thirds vote of the voting strength of the Board of Supervisors."[15]

The student of budgeting would have little pause in identifying the Nassau County budget as an executive budget. It is clearly the responsibility of the chief executive of the county. He prepares it, presents it, and administers it. Several observations might be advanced at this point. The position of budget director is unknown

[14] *Ibid.*, Sec. 305.
[15] *Ibid.*, Sec. 307.

in county government in Nassau. The review of estimates involves a considerable degree of assistance to the chief executive on the part of the comptroller and his staff. This practice of drawing on the manpower of the comptroller's office was initiated under the administration of the first county executive, J. Russell Sprague, who described it this way:

> Estimates are reviewed by the county executive before he makes his recommendations to the Board of Supervisors for the budget appropriations for the county. As a practical working arrangement, I caused reviews to be made by the two deputies of my office and by the county comptroller and his chief examiner of accounts. I personally checked the results of these reviews. I appreciate the many services extended to my office particularly in this connection by the county comptroller and the personnel of his office.[16]

As the functions of the county government continue to grow and the amounts of money being spent multiply, the pressures on the county executive increase and new techniques are required to help him do his job. One way would be to give the county executive a full-time director of the budget with an adequate staff to assist in the preparation and administration of the budget without the need for him to utilize the comptroller's staff to the extent that he now does.

Legislative consideration of the county budget resulted in no real alteration in the proposed budget for 1956. Perhaps the absence of changes means that the legislature is nothing more than a rubber stamp; or the situation provides an extraordinary example of executive–legislative harmony. Some might say that the board is inadequately staffed and lacks its own expert staff personnel to advise its members on budgetary matters. Maybe the unanimity stems from a combination of all three of these factors.

Revenue Administration

Revenue administration involves the determination of the value of property for tax purposes, the billing and collection of property taxes, and the collection of other types of revenue.

The county charter provides for a county Board of Assessors. Two are appointed from the most populous town and one from

[16] Nassau County, *Nassau County Government* (Mineola, 1940), p. 38.

each other town by the county executive with Board of Supervisors' approval for terms of four years. The chairman of the Board of Assessors is elected at large. Action is by majority vote. The board is charged with the duty of assessing "all property situated in the county and liable to taxation for state, county, town, school, and/or special district purposes."[17] The preparation of the assessment roll is the responsibility of the chairman of the Board of Assessors.

The Board of Assessors, following the hearing of complaints and the making of such corrections as are necessary in the assessment roll, transmits to the Board of Supervisors a statement of the total assessed valuation of the county and of each town, city, village, school district, and each special district and works benefit area. A similar statement of the assessed valuation of each city and village is sent to the respective government of each such unit. With the exception of eighteen villages all subdivisions of government in the county use the county assessment roll for purposes of local tax levies. The assessed valuations in Nassau County, as evident in Table 3 below, have steadily risen since 1945.

TABLE 3

Assessed Valuation of Property in Nassau County and All the Municipal Subdivisions Therein for the Years 1945, 1950, 1954

Unit of Government	1945	1950	1954
Nassau County	$1,097,942,665	$1,447,296,940	$1,903,663,193
Town of Hempstead	586,582,248	803,234,044	1,042,973,929
Town of N. Hempstead	290,450,273	373,352,057	467,588,649
Town of Oyster Bay	159,320,048	195,332,310	307,655,898
City of Glen Cove	29,043,933	33,129,600	38,251,264
City of Long Beach	32,547,163	42,248,929	47,193,453
Villages of:			
Baxter Estates	1,712,420	1,855,389	2,035,044
Bayville	5,559,938	6,792,141	7,622,299
Bellerose	3,511,800	3,610,087	3,801,954
Brookville	3,207,279	4,739,009	6,900,135
Cedarhurst	10,811,175	12,355,725	14,483,372
Centre Island	2,462,761	2,457,946	2,690,871
Cove Neck	2,675,424	2,734,411	2,565,880
East Hills	2,958,969	6,961,863	13,121,873
East Rockaway	10,215,558	15,259,280	18,202,895
East Williston	3,500,420	4,546,836	5,848,015
Farmingdale	6,650,665	7,246,040	9,810,300
Floral Park	25,075,956	26,828,763	31,347,166
Flower Hill	6,490,570	8,194,426	11,360,479

17 *County Government Law of Nassau County,* Art. VI, Sec. 602.

TABLE 3 *(cont.)*

Unit of Government	1945	1950	1954
Freeport	37,613,820	48,030,747	56,482,688
Garden City	48,613,122	59,163,051	72,189,174
Great Neck	22,687,656	16,240,015	37,727,295
Great Neck Est.	9,340,998	11,340,040	13,715,379
Great Neck Plaza	9,513,850	13,190,181	15,898,788
Hempstead	50,200,502	73,004,940	89,221,080
Hewlett Bay Park	2,408,680	2,947,680	3,352,135
Hewlett Harbor	1,890,734	2,938,630	6,095,602
Hewlett Neck	1,440,180	1,612,630	2,255,043
Island Park	3,623,849	3,148,479	3,849,107
Kensington	4,204,300	4,434,000	4,786,380
Kings Point	15,541,150	16,198,822	21,657,619
Lake Success	9,674,198	11,168,692	14,639,492
Lattingtown	7,530,581	7,561,332	8,197,610
Laurel Hollow	1,425,360	1,755,347	2,727,844
Lawrence	18,121,604	24,101,236	29,954,529
Lynbrook	32,590,675	39,954,950	46,351,000
Malverne	12,870,190	14,615,712	16,687,102
Manorhaven	2,591,384	4,022,199	4,384,947
Massapequa Park	1,590,260	3,745,594	13,811,054
Matinecock	5,200,165	5,561,320	6,470,515
Mill Neck	9,679,400	6,271,267	6,330,623
Mineola	20,212,407	27,226,340	35,447,570
Munsey Park	4,866,351	5,288,730	5,654,949
Muttontown	5,650,350	5,071,679	5,688,845
New Hyde Park	7,229,800	10,260,737	14,584,593
North Hills	4,170,085	4,141,535	4,567,970
Old Brookville	6,161,135	6,436,730	6,981,950
Old Westbury	16,616,130	15,068,250	17,207,080
Oyster Bay Cove	5,766,245	6,068,230	6,413,232
Plandome	5,005,759	5,196,474	5,471,324
Plandome Heights	1,255,387	2,752,515	2,900,785
Plandome Manor	2,545,594	2,778,899	3,328,684
Port Washington No.	———	1,120,145	1,150,220
Rockville Centre	40,063,544	46,264,217	58,337,797
Roslyn	3,179,380	4,331,522	7,040,642
Roslyn Estates	2,472,280	2,713,025	3,803,635
Roslyn Harbor	2,498,370	3,082,310	3,373,347
Russel Gardens	2,883,961	3,382,140	4,232,149
Saddle Rock	1,122,905	837,430	2,899,985
Sands Point	12,280,200	12,096,930	14,262,260
Sea Cliff	4,826,706	7,294,027	8,151,326
So. Floral Park	446,506	521,235	643,042
Stewart Manor	2,953,401	3,231,335	3,819,694
Thomaston	4,857,775	4,885,656	6,341,542
Upper Brookville	5,682,216	5,893,317	6,127,457
Valley Stream	31,417,460	39,606,590	54,252,785
Westbury	8,450,893	12,213,770	19,157,957
Williston Park	8,967,195	10,884,582	11,820,920
Woodsburgh	2,782,245	4,214,925	5,501,886

Source: Five-Year Cumulative Report of Nassau County, 1945, 1954. All figures rounded to the nearest dollar.

While the assessment function has been centralized to a considerable degree at the county level, the collection of property taxes involves several layers of government in the county. The county is charged with the collection of delinquent property taxes for the towns, the school districts, and all the special districts. The property taxes for county, state, Supreme Court, special districts, town, and school purposes are collected by the receivers of taxes of the three towns in the county.

The responsibility of the county for the collection of delinquent taxes for the towns, school districts, and all special districts does not presently place a significant financial burden on the government of the county since "Nassau's record of better than 99 per cent tax collection is the best in New York State."[18] This guarantee of a certain revenue to the smaller units of government does strengthen their financial position considerably.

The county treasurer, who is appointed by the county executive, receives and is the custodian of all money belonging to the county or in which the county has an interest. This activity includes the receipt and distribution of state aid, and collection of certain taxes in addition to delinquent property taxes.

The comptroller of Nassau County, elected from the county at large, is one of the most important officials in Nassau's governmental hierarchy. He is required to:

1. Keep and supervise all accounts.
2. Prescribe form of receipts, bills, claims, etc.
3. Examine and approve contracts, purchase orders, etc. by which the county incurs financial obligations.
4. Audit and approve all claims against the county.
5. Prepare monthly reports of all receipts and expenditures of the county.
6. "Examine and audit of his own motion or when directed to do so by resolution of the board of supervisors, the accounts and records of any town or special district and make reports from time to time when requested by the county executive or board of supervisors on the financial condition of the county or any of its political subdivisions."[19]

[18] Nassau County, *Your County Nassau* (Mineola, 1955).
[19] *County Government Law of Nassau County,* Art. IV, Sec. 402.

Each special district in the county must file with the comptroller, within sixty days after the conclusion of its fiscal year, an audit covering the financial operation of the fiscal year.

The county comptroller maintains accounts under a uniform system set forth by the state comptroller and is required to file an annual report to the state comptroller.

The head of the county Department of Purchase makes all purchases and contracts for any agency or department of the county. The county and state laws require the adherence to the standard procedures on competitive bidding, etc. followed in most centralized public purchasing programs.

We now turn our attention to the second level of government in the county, the towns.

B. THE TOWNS AND SPECIAL DISTRICTS

All of Nassau is divided into three towns, which are further divided into many districts.

Nassau County is divided into the towns of Hempstead, North Hempstead, and Oyster Bay. These three towns and their governments have roots deep in colonial American history. While Nassau was not set up as a county until 1899, and the first village, Hempstead, was not incorporated until 1853, these three towns were established prior to the adoption of the Constitution of the United States.

Each town consists of areas that are either incorporated as villages or cities or unincorporated. There are now sixty-three incorporated villages within the three towns, many of which are relatively small, highly restricted residential areas. While these villages provide legislative and service functions for their respective residents, they still rely on the towns for some services. The two cities in the county, Long Beach and Glen Cove, are beyond the jurisdiction of the town governments. The remaining area of the three towns is unincorporated and its governmental services are provided by town and special district administrations.

The characteristics of the three towns in terms of population, size, and location of incorporated and unincorporated areas are quite interesting and significant in understanding current problems and attempting to identify possible future demands for governmental services. It is clear from the map of the county, on page 22, that more than half of the incorporated areas in the three towns are located in the northern sections of the county; and that more than three-fourths of the villages and cities in the county are situated in the northern or western areas of Nassau. Approximately two-thirds of the villages have population of less than five thousand.[20] Villages with populations of more than five thousand seem to be concentrated in the western central part of the county. The majority of the people living in the three towns in Nassau reside in unincorporated areas and the population growth in the county is greatest in those parts of Nassau that are unincorporated, especially in the town of Oyster Bay. The population growth in the three towns since 1950 is estimated by the Long Island Lighting Company as shown in Table 4.

It should be noted that there is not a single incorporated jurisdiction, city or village, in Nassau, with a population of more than thirty-five thousand; yet there are two unincorporated areas with populations in the fifty thousand range and still growing.[21] Examination of the population figures for the five incorporated areas in the three towns that rank largest in population and the five unincorporated areas in the three towns that also rank highest in population, is most revealing.

Incorporated Area		Unincorporated Area	
Valley Stream	32,768	Levittown	52,110
Hempstead	32,303	East Meadow	47,303
Freeport	28,359	Hicksville	35,000
Rockville Centre	25,176	Valley Stream No. & So.	28,795
Glen Cove	19,296	Franklin Square	25,298

Each of the unincorporated areas of Levittown, East Meadow, and Hicksville has a population that exceeds that of the most heavily populated of the villages, Valley Stream. Moreover it should be noted that the largest city in the county, Glen Cove,

20 See Appendix A. Appendix C shows the area in square miles of each village in the county.

21 See Appendices A and B.

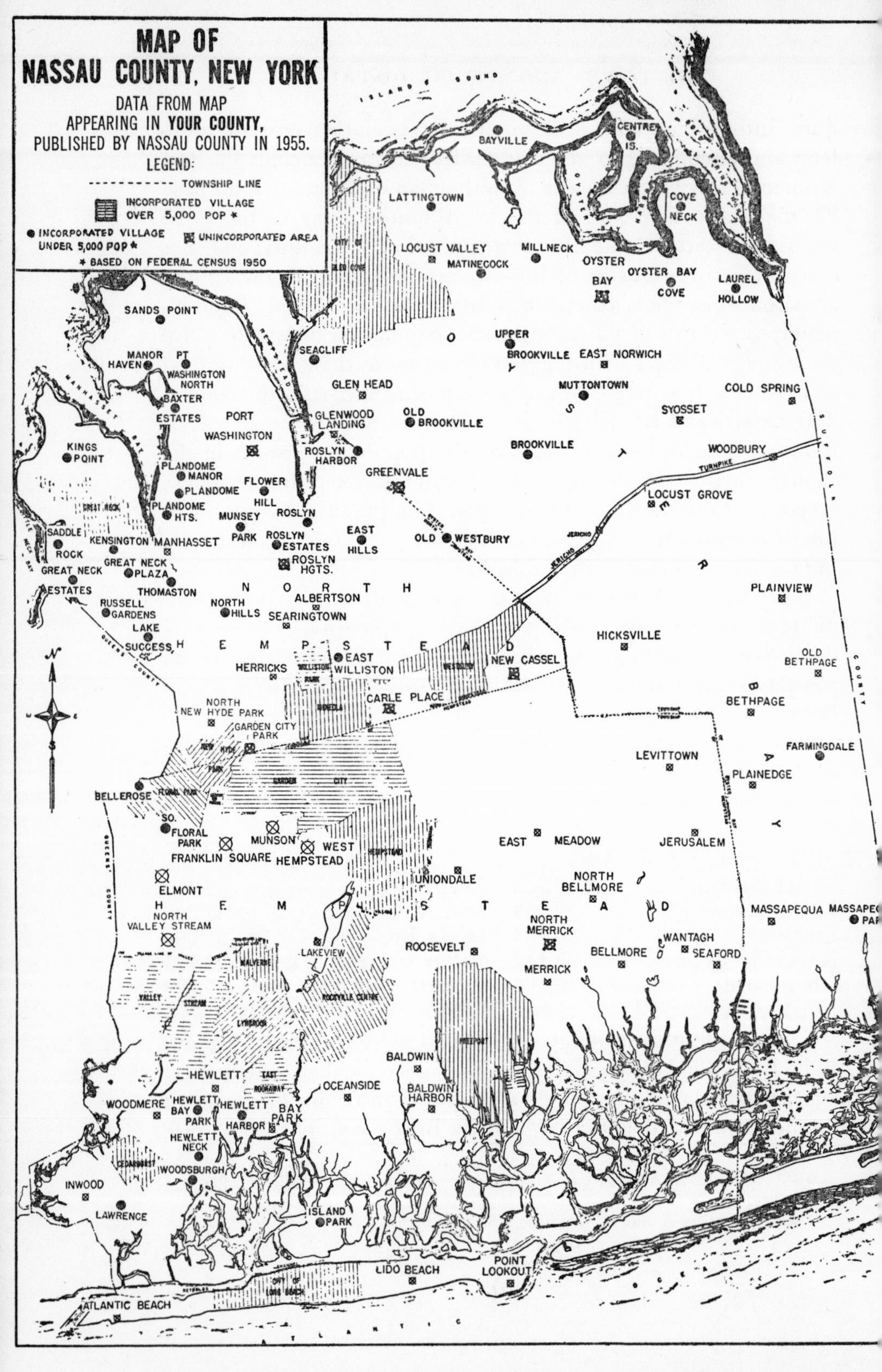
MAP OF
NASSAU COUNTY, NEW YORK
DATA FROM MAP
APPEARING IN YOUR COUNTY,
PUBLISHED BY NASSAU COUNTY IN 1955.
LEGEND:
TOWNSHIP LINE
INCORPORATED VILLAGE OVER 5,000 POP *
INCORPORATED VILLAGE UNDER 5,000 POP *
UNINCORPORATED AREA
* BASED ON FEDERAL CENSUS 1950
LONG ISLAND SOUND
BAYVILLE
CENTRE IS.
COVE NECK
LATTINGTOWN
LOCUST VALLEY
MATINECOCK
MILLNECK
OYSTER BAY
OYSTER BAY COVE
LAUREL HOLLOW
SANDS POINT
SEACLIFF
UPPER BROOKVILLE
EAST NORWICH
MANOR HAVEN
PT WASHINGTON NORTH
BAXTER ESTATES
PORT WASHINGTON
GLEN HEAD
MUTTONTOWN
COLD SPRING
GLENWOOD LANDING
OLD BROOKVILLE
SYOSSET
KINGS POINT
ROSLYN HARBOR
BROOKVILLE
WOODBURY
PLANDOME MANOR
GREENVALE
PLANDOME
FLOWER HILL
LOCUST GROVE
PLANDOME HTS.
MUNSEY PARK
ROSLYN
EAST HILLS
SADDLE ROCK
KENSINGTON
MANHASSET
ROSLYN ESTATES
OLD WESTBURY
GREAT NECK PLAZA
ROSLYN HGTS.
GREAT NECK ESTATES
THOMASTON
NORTH
ALBERTSON
PLAINVIEW
RUSSELL GARDENS
NORTH HILLS
SEARINGTOWN
HICKSVILLE
LAKE SUCCESS
HEMPSTEAD
EAST WILLISTON
HERRICKS
NEW CASSEL
OLD BETHPAGE
CARLE PLACE
BETHPAGE
NORTH NEW HYDE PARK
GARDEN CITY PARK
FARMINGDALE
LEVITTOWN
PLAINEDGE
BELLEROSE
SO. FLORAL PARK
MUNSON
WEST HEMPSTEAD
EAST MEADOW
JERUSALEM
FRANKLIN SQUARE
UNIONDALE
ELMONT
NORTH BELLMORE
NORTH VALLEY STREAM
NORTH MERRICK
MASSAPEQUA
WANTAGH
LAKEVIEW
ROOSEVELT
BELLMORE
SEAFORD
MERRICK
BALDWIN
HEWLETT
OCEANSIDE
BALDWIN HARBOR
WOODMERE
HEWLETT BAY PARK
HEWLETT HARBOR
BAY PARK
HEWLETT NECK
WOODSBURGH
INWOOD
LAWRENCE
ISLAND PARK
POINT LOOKOUT
LIDO BEACH
ATLANTIC BEACH
ATLANTIC OCEAN
SUFFOLK COUNTY
QUEENS COUNTY
OYSTER BAY
NORTH HEMPSTEAD
HEMPSTEAD
MANHASSET BAY
HEMPSTEAD HARBOR
JERICHO TURNPIKE
FREEPORT
ROCKVILLE CENTRE
LYNBROOK
VALLEY STREAM
MALVERNE
GARDEN CITY
MINEOLA
WESTBURY
FLORAL PARK
NEW HYDE PARK
CEDARHURST
EAST ROCKAWAY
CITY OF LONG BEACH
CITY OF GLEN COVE
GREAT NECK
WILLISTON PARK

TABLE 4

Population Estimate January 1, 1955

	Census 1950	LIL Est. 1/1/52	Increase Since Census		LIL Est. 1/1/54	Increase Since Census		LIL Est. 1/1/55	Increase Since Census	
			Number	Per Cent		Number	Per Cent		Number	Per Cent
NASSAU COUNTY										
Town of										
No. Hempstead	142613	166110	23497	16.48	184060	41447	29.06	190490	47877	33.57
Hempstead	448092	545040	96948	21.64	618070	169978	37.93	644560	196468	43.85
Oyster Bay	82060	119490	37430	45.61	164720	82660	100.73	197410	115350	140.57
Total	672765	830640	157875	23.47	966850	294085	43.71	1032460	359695	53.47

Source: Long Island Lighting Company, supplement to **Population Survey, 1954, Current Population Estimates for Nassau and Suffolk Counties** (Mineola, 1954).

with a population of 19,296 is exceeded in population by four villages and thirteen unincorporated areas.

The latter part of this section will concern itself with the government of the villages and the cities. Our attention is now directed to the town and special district governments, for these are the jurisdictions that are charged with providing the legislative, protection, and service functions for more than half of the population of the county.

Town Government

The three towns of Nassau County are governed under the provisions of the constitution of the state of New York, the town law, and various other state laws. With slight variations the town governments throughout the state are organized along very similar lines. The towns are divided into classes according to population. Hempstead, North Hempstead, and Oyster Bay are first-class towns. The town law treats quite specifically the nature and scope of the powers and duties of town officers, and it identifies the positions that make up the town government.

Given the fairly common pattern of town government throughout the county, it will suffice for us to examine the organizational structure of just one such unit, Hempstead. Governing the largest township in the state and the county, populationwise, the Hempstead town government operates within the framework of the organizational structure as identified on page 25.

It is readily apparent that town government does not reflect wholehearted acceptance of the principle of the short ballot, nor does it allow the town residents to pinpoint responsibility for town services on a strong chief executive.

The presiding supervisor, elected for two years, is the chief administrative officer of the township and presides at board meetings as well as representing the town on the county Board of Supervisors. Hempstead has two supervisors since its population exceeds that of the balance of the county.[22]

The Town Board, consisting of the two supervisors and four

[22] North Hempstead and Oyster Bay have only one supervisor. *Town Law,* Sec. 41.

GOVERNMENTAL CHART

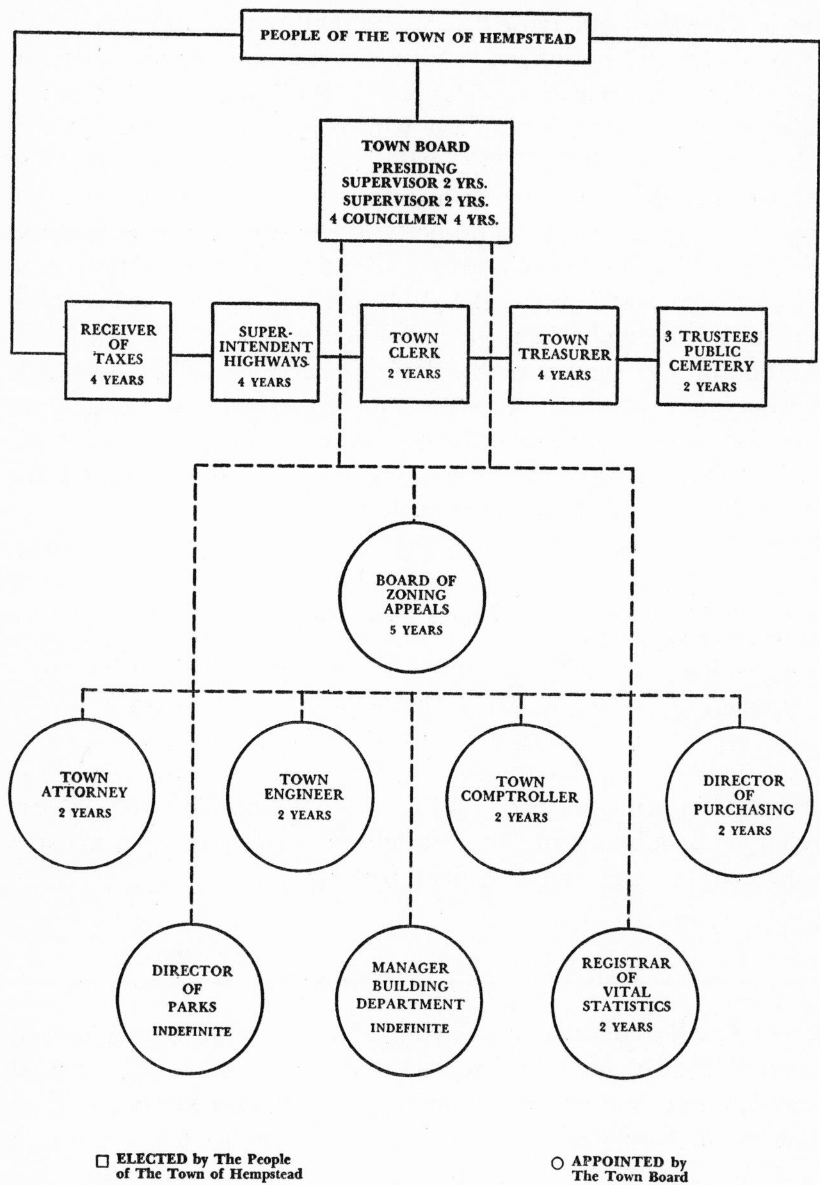

SOURCE: Town of Hempstead, *Hempstead, Nassau County*.

town councilmen, is vested "with all the powers of such a town and shall continue to have and to exercise such powers until the legislature shall otherwise direct, and shall possess and exercise all the powers and be subject to all the duties now or hereafter imposed by law upon town boards."[23] The Town Board may not abridge or interfere in any way with the power and authority of the villages and cities within its limits. The general powers of the board include control of town finances; acquisition of real property; management of town property; the letting of contracts, granting franchises over public streets; adopting town ordinances; general matters pertaining to the public health, welfare, and safety of the people living in the town, and other powers. The Town Board is the administrative as well as the legislative body of the town government. A majority of the members of the Town Board are elected every two years. The two supervisors are elected every two years, and two of the four councilmen, elected for four years, are chosen at each biennial election.

Town Finance

The fiscal year of all towns begins on the first day of January and ends on the thirty-first of December. The chief fiscal officer of the town is the supervisor.[24] The other fiscal officers of the town are the following: the town clerk, the comptroller, the receiver of taxes, the town treasurer, and the Town Board. These officials are charged with budgeting, revenue administration, treasury management, accounting, and financial reporting.

The Town Budget

Unlike the county budget system, that of the towns does not provide in the law for an executive budget, prepared by the chief administrative officer and presented by him to the Town Board for adoption. Under the terms of the town law the town budget is prepared, presented, and adopted in the following manner:

[23] *Town Law,* Sec. 60.
[24] In the case of Hempstead, the presiding supervisor.

1. Estimates of expenditures and anticipated revenues are filed by every administrative officer, board, department, and commission of every district therein with the town clerk between the 20th and 30th day of September in each year.

2. On or before the 5th day of October the town clerk is charged by the law to "present such detailed estimates to the board."[25]

3. Between the 5th and 10th days of October the Town Board is required to prepare and approve the preliminary budget, an itemized statement in writing of the estimated revenues and expenditures of the town for the next fiscal year. The town law specifies just what the estimates of revenue and expenditure must contain. The law further provides that the "town board shall also include in such statement and separately set forth similar estimates of revenues and expenditures for each improvement or other district in the town . . . but the town board shall make no change in the estimate of revenues and expenditures submitted by the board of fire commissioners of any fire district."[26]

4. On or before the Thursday immediately following the general election, a public hearing is held. "At such hearing, any person may be heard in favor of or against the preliminary budget as compiled or for or against any item or items therein contained. or to the indebtedness of the town."[27] The Town Board adopts such preliminary budget as originally compiled or it may, by a majority vote of its members, diminish or reject any item or items therein contained, except those relating to a fire district or to the estimated revenue or to the indebtedness of the town or any district therein, but it shall not have the power to increase any item of the estimated expenditures, except those relating to highways or to the indebtedness of the town."[27] The Town Board adopts the preliminary budget as amended.

5. Emergency appropriations over and above the budget may be made during the course of the fiscal year, providing that the board adopts a resolution by a two-thirds vote declaring an emergency exists.

6. The town clerk must give a copy of the adopted budget to

[25] *Town Law,* Sec. 111.
[26] *Town Law,* Sec. 112.
[27] *Town Law,* Sec. 113.

the supervisor of the town, who in turn presents it to the county Board of Supervisors. "The board of supervisors shall levy and cause to be raised the amounts specified in said annual budget to be levied by tax or assessments, and such amounts shall be levied, assessed and raised by tax and assessments upon the real property of the town liable therefor."[28]

The town law of New York State does not specifically identify any town official as the single executive responsible for the preparation, submission, and administration of the town budget. Instead the law simply requires the department heads to file their budget estimates with the town clerk and charges the town board with the preparation and adoption of an "itemized statement" or a budget. What seems on the surface to be an outmoded budget system is not quite as bad as it might be. The author's conversations with Hempstead officials have left the impression that the presiding supervisor of the town exercises to a limited degree somewhat more of the functions of a chief executive in the budget process than is discernible from just reading the law. The practice seems to be for the various town department and agency heads to submit their budget requests to the supervisor's office, following what might be called executive budget hearings; the budget requests are then filed with the town clerk, who presents the budget to the board. No budget message accompanies the budget document.

The town comptroller, who is appointed, exercises day-to-day control over town expenditures. "The Comptroller's records show on any given day just how much has been spent and how much remains in each departmental budget. They show the condition of the town's general fund, the special district funds and all subdivisions in the respective funds. All accounts, charges, claims or demands against the town are examined, audited, allowed or rejected by the Comptroller."[29] The comptroller annually audits the fiscal affairs of each improvement district.

The receiver of taxes, elected for a four-year term, receives and collects all state, county, town, special district, and school taxes

[28] *Town Law*, Sec. 116.
[29] Town of Hempstead, *Hempstead, Nassau County*, 1955.

within the town. The individual incorporated area tax is the only tax levied in the county that is not collected by the receiver of taxes.

The property owners in the unincorporated parts of the town in Nassau County receive two separate tax bills from the receiver of taxes. One is a consolidated levy covering the Supreme Court, the county highways, police, and special districts. The other is the school tax bill. The first tax bill is sent to each property owner in the town with a brief statement explaining how the consolidated rate appearing on the tax bill is arrived at. The property owner pays a consolidated tax rate representing the total of all the tax rates of every district that provides his property with services. In the unincorporated areas the number of districts levying a tax on property is considerably greater than in the incorporated areas. Hence the consolidated tax rate on the town tax bill covering state, county, town, and special districts is usually higher in an unincorporated village. The village resident, however, receives an additional tax bill, the village tax bill, that the property owner in the unincorporated area does not. The second tax bill, the school tax, is sent to each property owner in the town. The tax rate, as in the case of each special district, is different from school district to school district. The school tax rates and the school budgets are set by the local school boards. The town is merely the collection agent. The total impact of these taxes in terms of the unincorporated area and the incorporated area is worth a brief review.

In one unincorporated area of the town of Hempstead a property owner received a 1955 tax bill with a consolidated tax rate of $3.638 per $100 of assessed valuation. On the face of his bill under the heading of Rate Code he found the numbers of the districts which provided him with governmental services. They were listed as follows:

Rate Code

1 2 3 8 49 80 93 202 X C

As the list of special districts and their various 1955 tax rates

TABLE 5

List of Special Districts and Summary of the Various Tax Rates of the Town of Hempstead for the Tax Levy of 1955

District Number		Rate per $100. Assd. Valuation	
1	State, Court	$ .008	
	County	1.326	
	Town—General Purposes	.00	
			$1.334
2	Town Highway—Repairs and Improvements of Highways		.31
3	Nassau County Police		.427
	Water Districts		
4	Bethpage		.11
5	Franklin Square		.076
6	Hicksville		.095
7	Uniondale		.35
8	West Hempstead-Hempstead Gardens		.07
9	East Meadow		.271
16	Garden City South		.085
124	Island Trees		.047
125	Bowling Green Estates		.29
126	Levittown		.127
T	Lido-Pt. Lookout		.492
	Water Supply Districts		
11	Bellmore		.066
12	Bellmore Plaza		.101
13	Clear Brook Park		.00
14	East Lawrence		.035
15	Elmont		.085
17	Inwood		.046
18	Lakeview		.086
19	Lawrence North		.051
20	Meadowmere		.05
21	Merrick		.055
22	No. Lynbrook		.146
23	Roosevelt		.086
24	Malverne Park		.025
	Lighting Districts		
25	Central Park		.271
26	Baldwin		.115
27	Baldwin Harbor		.082
28	Barnum Island		.295
29	Bay Park		.116
30	Clear Stream		.04
31	East Hempstead		.077
32	East Lawrence		.019
33	East Meadow		.143
34	Elmont		.116
35	Franklin Square		.096
36	Hempstead Gardens		.093
37	Inwood		.112
38	Lakeview		.097
39	Lawrence North		.074
40	Lido-Pt. Lookout		.086
41	Malverne		.091
42	Meadowmere		.072
43	Merrick		.098
44	Oceanside		.104
45	Roosevelt		.142
46	South Hempstead		.118
47	Southside		.16
48	Harbor Isle		.084
49	West Hempstead		.089
50	West Long Beach		.059
51	Woodlawn Terrace		.053
52	Woodmere		.067
53	Hewlett-Woodmere		.099
54	Green Acres		.105
154	Island Trees		.226
155	Bowling Green Estates		.157
	Fire Districts		
55	Bethpage		.133
56	Baldwin		.364
57	Barnum Island		.275
58	Bay Park		.19
59	Bellerose Terrace		.424
60	Bellmore		.259
61	East End-Atlantic Beach		.201
62	East Meadow		.293
63	Elmont		.126
64	Franklin Square-Munson		.137
65	Hewlett Bay		.231
66	Inwood		.379
67	Lakeview		.233
68	Lawrence North		.186
69	Lido-Pt. Lookout		.182
70	New Hyde Park		.244
71	North Bellmore		.273
72	North Merrick		.209
73	Oceanside		.299
74	Roosevelt		.421
75	Seaford		.323
76	South Hempstead		.565
77	Uniondale		.374

TABLE 5 *(cont.)*

District Number		Rate per $100. Assd. Valuation
78	Wantagh	.194
79	West End-Atlantic Beach	.19
80	West Hempstead	.228
81	Woodmere	.18
112	Levittown	.269
	Fire Protection Districts	
82	Green Acres	.155
83	East Garden City	.11
84	East Lawrence	.141
85	North West Malverne	.104
86	Roosevelt Field	.101
87	Merrick	.145
88	South Westbury	.106
89	Angle Sea	.109
90	South Franklin Square	.106
102	South Hempstead	.149
103	Wreck Lead	.318
104	South Barnum Island	.59
106	Hempstead Plains	.148
108	South Bellmore	.101
116	Meadowmere	.251
117	West Sunbury	.188
121	South East Hempstead	.104
127	East End Atlantic Beach	.234
	Sanitary Districts	
91	District No. 1	.45
92	District No. 2	.483
93	District No. 6	.529
94	District No. 7	.553
95	District No. 14	.304
	Refuse and Garbage Districts	
96	Bay Park-Hewlett Point	.759
109	North Lynbrook	.489
113	Lido-Pt. Lookout	.42
114	Barnum Island	.456
115	Bowling Green Estates	.498
128	Harbor Isle	.539
L	Levittown	.563
	Refuse Disposal	
X	Town of Hempstead Refuse Disposal	.059

District Number				Rate per $100. Assd. Valuation
	Sea Wall Assmt. Area			
105	Point Lookout			.00
	Beach Protection Area			
S	Atlantic Beach			.704
	Park Districts			
100	Point Lookout			.419
101	East Atlantic Beach			1.038
110	Lido Beach			1.56
118	Levittown			.11
120	Atlantic Beach			.673
P	Hempstead-Oyster Bay Hall & Pools			.173
	Town Sewer Districts			
97	Green Acres			Assmt. Basis
99	West Long Beach			Assmt. Basis
	County Sewer District			
202	Nassau County Sewer Disposal No. 2 Bonds and Interest (Construction)			.167
	Sewer Collection Districts			
		[1] No. 1	**[2] No. 2**	
A	2-V.S.	.052	.45	.502
B	2-B.	.052	.474	.526
C	2-F.S.	.052	.373	.425
D	2-F.P.	.052	.225	.277
E	2-W.H.	.052	.335	.387
F	R.I.A.	.00	.432	.432
H	2-N.H.P.	.052	.00	.052
	Parking Districts			
10	Baldwin Public			.059
107	Franklin Square Public			.664
119	Merrick Public			.048
129	Woodmere-Hewlett Public			.068
R	Roosevelt Public			.026

[1] No. 1: Operation and Maintenance Costs of Sewer Disposal District No. 2 within the Collection Districts.

[2] No. 2: Operation and Maintenance Costs of Collection Districts.

shown in Table 5 indicates, the figure $3.638 represents the total of:

	District No.	Rate per $100
Armory and Court Expense	1	$ .008
County		1.326
Town—General Purpose		.00
Town Highway	2	.31
Nassau County Police	3	.427
Water District	8	.07
Lighting District	49	.089
Fire District	80	.228
Sanitary District	93	.529
Refuse Disposal	X	.059
County Sewer District	202	.167
Sewer Collection District	C	.425
Total Consolidated tax for services of 10 separate districts		$3.638

This particular piece of property is also located within the boundaries of school district number 27. The tax rate for this district for the 1955–1956 school year was $4.260.[30] The owner of this property in an unincorporated area paid the town receiver of taxes the first bill of $3.638 per $100 assessment for the services identified above and the second tax bill of $4.260 per $100 for schools or a total tax of $7.898 per $100 of assessed valuation for governmental services, except education, for the fiscal period January through December 1955. The school tax covers the educational services over a twelve-month period spanning 1955 and 1956.

In contrast, the owner of a piece of property in an incorporated village received a 1955 town tax bill with a consolidated tax rate of $1.501 per $100 of assessed valuation. The numbers of the districts in which his property is subject to taxes were identified under the Rate Code 1 202. As shown in Table 5, 1 represents a tax of $.008 plus $1.326 or $1.334; and 202 has a tax rate of $.167 for a total consolidated tax of $1.501 per $100 of assessed valuation. This property is in school district 18. The tax rate for district 18 for the 1955–1956 school year was $2.780. Hence the resident of the incorporated area sent the town receiver of taxes two separate

[30] See Table 6.

payments with the two bills sent him by the town, the total amount being $4.281 per $100 of assessed valuation. One should not assume, however, that the property owner of the incorporated area paid only $4.281 per $100 assessed valuation while the owner in the unincorporated area paid a total rate of $7.898 for similar services. The figure $7.898 represents the sum total of all the rates (1955–1956) of all the local jurisdictions in the county which are entitled to levy a tax on the property in the unincorporated area. The property owner in the incorporated village must first add another tax rate to the $4.281, namely the village tax rate per $100 of assessed valuation, before any comparison of total tax rates between an incorporated and an unincorporated area is possible.

The village tax rate for the above-mentioned property for the fiscal year March 1955 through February 1956 was $1.79 per $100 of assessed valuation. This means that in this particular year the property owner in the incorporated area paid $6.071 per $100 for all his local governmental services, while the property owner in the particular unincorporated area considered above paid nearly $2 per $100 of assessed valuation more or $7.898 for the same kinds of services, but not necessarily the same quality of service.

Special Districts

In 1956 there were approximately 260 special districts in Nassau County. The growth in the number of special districts, from 87 in 1920, to 173 in 1933, to almost one hundred more in 1955, has paralleled the growth of the population in the county's unincorporated areas.

The listing in Table 7 of special districts indicates the range of services the resident of the unincorporated area receives from a variety of governmental units. His fire protection is provided by one kind of district, his water by another, his garbage collection by another, his lighting by still another, and so on. As indicated earlier, the resident is billed for these services by the town in the form of a consolidated tax bill. The cost of the services rendered to the resident of the special district is levied on the inhabitants of that particular district and not upon others in the larger com-

TABLE 6

Town of Hempstead, 1954–1955 School Tax Levy

School District	Assessed Valuation	Taxes Levied	Estimated State Aid	Tax Rate
1—Hempstead	$73,659,435	$1,546,850.24	$ 878,083.55	$2.10
2—Uniondale	49,805,680	1,424,442.72	560,158.46	2.86
3—East Meadow	61,703,716	1,801,749.41	1,470,500.00	2.92
4—No. Bellmore	24,659,675	949,412.11	575,387.00	3.85
5—Levittown	63,193,651	2,319,237.49	2,137,467.85	3.67
6—Seaford	17,268,185	607,839.60	255,100.00	3.52
7—Bellmore	11,598,295	499,892.26	166,314.14	4.31
8—Roosevelt	17,074,192	471,247.57	210,000.00	2.76
9—Freeport	54,141,130	1,553,867.82	606,250.00	2.87
10—Baldwin	45,005,695	1,458,184.54	812,221.92	3.24
11—Oceanside	46,635,550	1,632,253.17	823,155.00	3.50
12—Malverne	26,999,910	737,106.93	403,000.00	2.73
13—N. Valley Stream	43,728,585	1,604,857.86	650,000.00	3.67
14—Hewlett-Woodmere	42,743,595	1,610,152.20	358,163.35	3.767
15—Law'nce-Ced'st-Inw'd	72,814,764	2,172,791.55	554,600.00	2.984
16—Elmont	59,011,891	1,947,398.26	1,076,982.00	3.30
17—Franklin Sq.	35,643,525	1,286,748.34	563,035.00	3.61
18—Garden City	67,231,490	1,559,770.86	250,000.00	2.32
19—E. Rockaway	13,231,270	387,682.75	202,240.00	2.93
20—Lynbrook	38,008,945	1,254,296.59	376,181.84	3.30
21—Rockville Centre	54,714,900	1,630,504.18	486,552.14	2.98
22—Floral Pk.-B'lerose	32,950,130	929,193.79	230,000.00	2.82
23—Wantagh	22,872,230	1,017,826.27	405,057.00	4.45
24—Valley Stream	22,940,520	837,338.75	156,303.10	3.65
25—Merrick	22,027,580	940,586.22	275,000.00	4.27
26—Island Trees	20,604,030	712,899.61	551,375.00	3.46
27—W. Hempstead	28,872,370	1,019,206.02	468,929.15	3.53
28—Long Beach	63,044,292	1,657,437.23	483,922.21	2.629[2]
29—No. Merrick	17,123,585	714,062.52	340,000.00	4.17
30—Valley Stream	23,186,950	788,356.30	301,000.00	3.40
31—Island Park	8,543,084	206,743.48	60,000.00	2.42
NH 1—Westbury	208,640	5,654.30	368,000.00[1]	2.71
NH 5—New Hyde Pk.	3,996,165	118,006.75	450,000.00[1]	2.953
	$1,185,243,655	$37,403,597.69	$17,504,978.71	

[1] Estimated State Aid for entire District, including Portion in Town of North Hempstead.
[2] Library Rate $.071 included.

TABLE 6 *(cont.)*

Town of Hempstead, 1955–1956 School Tax Levy

School District	Assessed Valuation	Taxes Levied	Estimated State Aid	Tax Rate
1	$80,942,943	$1,844,550.67	$ 857,295.43	$2.280
2	52,147,135	1,661,434.07	710,400.09	3.190
3	67,274,838	2,302,512.08	2,229,775.00	3.423
4	27,104,140	1,043,524.34	501,789.00	3.850
5	66,334,411	3,084,474.63	2,256,000.00	4.650
6	19,802,190	734,631.34	304,368.72	3.714
7	12,002,050	495,507.10	120,000.00	4.140
8	18,943,512	647,868.74	240,000.00	3.420
9	56,743,788	1,654,082.05	650,000.00	2.920
10	47,095,640	1,572,193.53	868,889.00	3.340
11	50,048,595	1,968,068.24	950,125.00	3.940
12	27,579,374	866,133.25	410,700.00	3.150
13	45,611,278	2,073,761.91	815,000.00	4.550
14	44,542,383	1,922,173.70	403,100.00	4.320
15	76,847,829	2,478,889.93	578,000.00	3.230
16	61,688,892	2,344,012.34	875,898.00	3.800
17	37,506,560	1,571,542.65	710,787.00	4.190
18	72,822,202	2,016,579.38	300,000.00	2.780
19	13,521,934	403,745.80	211,000.00	2.990
20	39,272,887	1,220,260.21	619,199.58	3.130
21	55,711,285	1,901,824.38	531,501.32	3.420
22	33,601,261	1,016,687.72	165,000.00	3.040
23	24,529,845	1,077,277.51	538,658.02	4.400
24	24,254,817	1,117,950.31	179,596.00	4.700
25	22,772,315	946,033.23	222,400.00	4.160
26	21,743,605	960,982.27	820,161.94	4.420
27	30,555,100	1,298,436.54	522,111.00	4.260
28	65,455,964	1,834,074.29	500,028.03	2.806 [2]
29	18,211,297	797,655.43	302,702.82	4.380
30	24,429,573	1,124,016.61	340,000.00	4.610
31	9,881,265	282,259.19	75,000.00	2.875
NH 1	243,075	6,636.05	382,500.00 [1]	2.730
NH 5	4,135,668	150,368.23	345,000.00 [1]	3.654
	$1,253,357,651	$44,420,147.72	$19,536,985.95	

[1] Estimated State Aid for entire District, including Portion in Town of North Hempstead.
[2] Library Rate .0913 included.

munity of the town who do not directly benefit from the special district activities or services.

These special districts are created under the provisions of the town law. The procedure calls for the filing of a petition with the town board by the owners of taxable real property amounting to at least 50 per cent of the assessed valuation of all the taxable real property of the proposed special district. Following a public hearing on the petition, the board is required, among other things, to determine "whether it is in the public interest to grant in whole or in part the relief sought."[31] If the board decides all is in order

TABLE 7

Special Districts as of August 1955

Kind of District	Hempstead	North Hempstead	Oyster Bay	Total
Fire	28	5	8	41
Fire Protection	18	8	8	34
Fire Hydrant Rental			1	1
Garbage		7	21	28
Lighting Districts	32	12	12	56
Parks	6	3	3	12
Parking, Paving, & Improvement	8	1	7	16
Police District		1		1
Refuse and Sanitary	13			13
Sewer	3	3	1	7
Water	24	11	14	49
Drainage District			1	1
	132	51	76	259

1 County
3 Towns
2 Cities
63 Villages
62 School Districts 34, 11, 27
259 Special Districts

390 Units of Government
+9 {1 County Police District
1 County Sewage Disposal No. 2
7 County Collection Districts}

399

Source: Report on Assessed Valuation, Department of Assessment, County of Nassau, August 12, 1955 (mimeo).

[31] *Town Law,* Sec. 171.

and acts in the affirmative, the district is set up. Often, such action by the board is then subject to review and approval by the state comptroller. The town files an application with the state comptroller for permission to create a district.

> The State Comptroller shall within five days thereafter give notice thereof to the board of supervisors of the county in which such proposed district or extension is located by filing with the clerk of such board of supervisors one copy of such application. At any time within 15 days of the filing of the application, the board of supervisors may file an objection, in writing, in the office of the department of audit and control. In addition, the State Comptroller shall determine whether the public interest will be served by the creation or extension of the district and also whether the cost thereof will be an undue burden upon the property of the proposed district or extension.[32]

The permission of the state comptroller is not usually required in the establishment or extension of a district unless such action involves financing the cost thereof by the issuance of bonds, notes, or other evidences of indebtedness of the town.

Some of the special districts are run by elected commissioners; others are administered by the Town Board. Those which are run by the Town Board are primarily taxing districts. Those districts which have special commissioners have responsibility for the financial affairs of the district. "But, regardless of the system of administration, the financial affairs of the district are closely associated with those of the town."[33]

In the town of Hempstead, the following kinds of special districts have elected commissioners: [34]

District	Number
Fire	28
Sanitation	5
Water	4
Sewer	1
Total	38

[32] *Town Law,* Sec. 194, 3b.

[33] M. P. Catherwood, T. N. Hurd, and C. A. Bratton, *Rural Government in New York.* New York State College of Agriculture, Cornell University (Ithaca, 1947), p. 4.

[34] Interview with town official, April 1956.

Those special districts run by the Town Board are:[35]

District	Number
Fire Protection	18
Lighting	32
Park	6
Parking	6
Refuse and Garbage	7
Refuse Disposal	1
Sewer	1
Water	6
Water Supply	13
Improvement	2
Total	92

In the fire districts, the elected commissioners annually prepare and file, in the office of the town clerk of each town, estimates of revenue and expenditures for the fiscal year. The Town Board can make no change in the estimate submitted by the board of fire commissioners of any fire district. The taxes are collected by the town and paid to the fire commission of each district. The law requires that "the Treasurer of each fire district shall prepare and file annually in the office of the town clerk of each town in which any part of such fire district shall be located, and in the office of the State Comptroller, a financial statement setting forth in detail the receipts and expenditures of such fire districts."[36] Other districts with elected commissioners, including some of the water districts, have a comparable degree of freedom in the preparation and administration of their budgets.

The ninety-two special districts in the town which are run by the Town Board have their budgets prepared and administered in roughly the same way as the various town departments operating under the Town Board and the presiding supervisor have theirs prepared.

There is no comprehensive program of centralized purchasing, to the author's knowledge, that places all purchasing for the town and every special district therein in one office.

[35] *Ibid.*

[36] *Town Law,* Art. 71, Sec. 81.

The author was unable to locate a map of the county that showed the various boundary lines of all the local units of government. Nor does it seem possible to prepare one. One report on Nassau prepared in 1933 when Nassau had more than 173 special districts states that:

> A description of the number and variety of special districts has already been given. One cannot examine these facts without bias and avoid the conclusion that there are far too many. They are crowded against each other and piled in layers on top of each other. Their boundary lines do not, in most cases, correspond with any natural or logical demarcation of territory to be administered. They just grew without regard for any plan as the need for services became manifest.[37]

The report continues: "As the county grows and becomes more thoroughly urban in character the need for special districts as administrative units will diminish. As a matter of fact, conditions have already reached the point where some kinds of districts can be eliminated."[38] The need may have begun diminishing in 1933 but the number of special districts has been steadily increasing ever since.

While special districts have been increasing at the rate of six or seven a year since 1945, the number of incorporated areas, villages, and cities has remained constant. To these jurisdictions we now turn our attention.

C. NASSAU'S INCORPORATED AREAS

There are sixty-three incorporated villages and two cities in Nassau County. They vary widely in size, population, date of incorporation, and range of governmental services provided.

The majority of the villages and the two cities were set up in the period between the end of World War I and the depression year of 1932. Hempstead was the first village in the county to become incorporated. This was in 1853. No village or city has been incorporated since 1932. Areawise, the villages run from one-tenth of a square mile (Bellerose) to nine square miles (Old Westbury).

37 Municipal Consultant Service of the National Municipal League, *op. cit.*, p. 60.
38 *Ibid.*, p. 62.

More than one-third of the incorporated areas, 24, cover areas of less than one square mile each.[39] Nineteen villages cover an area of between 1 and 1.9 square miles. Seven villages and the city of Long Beach are between 2 and 2.9 square miles in size. Six villages are between 2.9 and 3.9 square miles in size and four are between 4 and 5 square miles; one covers 5.3 square miles; the city of Glen Cove covers 6.6 square miles and Old Westbury covers 9 square miles. In other words, one-third of the incorporated areas are less than one square mile in size, two-thirds are under two square miles, and roughly 90 per cent are under four square miles in total area for each village.

The population of the villages and the cities also represents a wide range,[40] from 212 in Cove Neck to 32,768 in Valley Stream. The breakdown of localities according to population is as follows:

TABLE 8

Population	No. of Villages and Cities
Below 500	8
500– 1,000	16
1,000– 1,500	6
2,000– 3,000	10
3,000– 4,000	2
4,000– 5,000	2
5,000– 6,000	3
6,000– 7,000	1
7,000– 8,000	1
8,000– 9,000	1
9,000–10,000	3
10,000–11,000	0
11,000–12,000	1
17,000–18,000	2
18,000–19,000	2
19,000–20,000	2
25,000–26,000	1
28,000–29,000	1
32,000–33,000	2

Twenty-four, or more than one-third, of the villages have a population of fewer than 1,000. Forty-two or nearly two-thirds of the

39 See Appendix C.
40 See Appendix A.

TABLE 9

Rank	By Population	By Size
1	Valley Stream	Old Westbury
2	Hempstead	Glen Cove
3	Freeport	Garden City
4	Rockville Centre	Freeport
5	Glen Cove	Lawrence
6	Mineola	Upper Brookville
7	Lynbrook	Sands Point
8	Garden City	Muttontown
9	Long Beach	Hempstead
10	Floral Park	Valley Stream
11	Westbury	Kings Point
12	New Hyde Park	Brookville
13	Great Neck	North Hills
14	Malverne	Rockville Centre
15	East Rockaway	Mill Neck

villages have fewer than 4,000. Fifty of the 65 incorporated areas have a population of fewer than 9,000. Ten are between 9 and 20 thousand and only four above the 20,000 figure.

Those villages that have the largest population are not necessarily the ones that cover the widest area in square miles. For example, the largest village in square miles, Old Westbury, 9 square miles, has a population of just 1,261, while the smallest village areawise, Bellerose, one square mile, has a population of 115 less or 1,146.

The ranking of the 15 largest incorporated areas according to population and area is shown in Table 9 above. Only six of the names appear in both columns.

TABLE 10

Rank	By Population	By Area
1	Cove Neck	Bellerose
2	Laurel Hollow	Plandome Heights
3	Centre Island	Russell Gardens
4	North Hills	Baxter Estates
5	Plandome Manor	Hewlett Neck
6	Brookville	Kensington
7	Muttontown	South Floral Park
8	Hewlett Neck	Stewart Manor
9	Hewlett Bay Park	Island Park
10	Roslyn Harbor	Great Neck Estates

Table 10 shows the ranking of the 10 smallest incorporated areas by population and area.

At this end of the scale, only one name appears on both lists.

Under the state law, villages are divided into classes according to their population as shown by the last enumeration, as follows:

First Class	5,000 or more
Second Class	3,000–5,000
Third Class	1,000–3,000
Fourth Class	Up to 1,000

The powers and activities of the first class villages are greater than those of the smaller units.

Cities and Villages

The incorporated villages in Nassau elect a mayor and a Board of Trustees consisting of 2 to 6 members. The mayor serves as the executive officer. The board performs all legislative functions, appropriates funds, and determines all questions of policy and matters of procedure. The village boards zone, license, issue building permits, and in some cases maintain highway, police, and other departments. The range of village activities varies from village to village. The only other elected village official is the police justice. This office is required for first class villages as are the appointive positions of treasurer and village clerk for all activities.

One of the village governments generally recognized as better than average is that of Garden City, which is a first class village. The mayor and six trustees are elected to serve terms of two years. "At the annual organization meeting of the Board, the Mayor assigns the trustees as commissioners of various departments to supervise their operations. They report on their department activities at each Board meeting."[41] Thus in 1955 an unsalaried trustee served as a responsible administrator in the following capacities:

1. Acting Mayor and Commissioner of Parks and Public Buildings
2. Police Commissioner

[41] *Annual Report of the Incorporated Village of Garden City* (1955), p. 11.

3. Commissioner of Public Works
4. Fire Commissioner
5. Commissioner of Water Supply, Saftey, and Insurance
6. Comptroller and Commissioner of Purchases

The Board of Trustees appoints five members to the Board of Review, which passes upon plans of residential buildings submitted by builders; designates five persons to sit as a Board of Appeals to consider applications for variances from the zoning laws; and creates a five-man planning commission "who pass upon plans to develop vacant areas, streets, parks and other public places."[42] Other appointed village officials include the village clerk, the village counsel and the village treasurer. A police justice is elected for four years.

Financial Management at the Municipal Level

Villages and cities are creatures of the state. Their powers in fiscal affairs are clearly identified in the many provisions of the state constitution, state legislation and administrative regulations. Village taxing and village borrowing are limited by law.[43] Budgeting and accounting procedures are closely supervised by the state comptroller's office, and each local unit of government is required to file an annual report with that office. The fiscal year for villages in New York State may start on one of three possible dates, June 1, August 1, or March 1.[44]

The management of municipal finance involves the usual functions of revenue administration, accounting and financial reporting, purchasing as well as budgeting. The treasurer of a village is its chief fiscal officer. He has custody of all moneys belonging to the village and keeps accounts of all receipts and expenditures in conformance with a uniform system of accounts prescribed by the state comptroller. He must also render reports on the financial status of the village affairs.

The village clerk in Garden City is also the village assessor.

42 *Ibid.*, p. 11.
43 See Appendix E.
44 *Village Law*, Sec. 117, 1955.

Garden City is one of the eighteen villages in the county that do not use the county rolls for village tax purposes but prepare their own tax rolls. The Garden City village clerk "records the proceedings and decisions of the Trustees and all of the village units. He is responsible for the accounting of all village finances, preparation of assessment rolls, billing and collecting taxes and other charges, and maintaining records. He records all vital statistics, permits and licenses."[45]

All village purchasing in Garden City, with the exception of the offices of the village clerk and the treasurer, is handled by the Department of Public Works. State law requires advertisement and sealed bids on all purchases over $1,000.

The financial operations of the village are carefully reviewed each year.

> Certified Public Accountants annually audit the accounts and records of the village. Their report is submitted to the Board of Trustees. Detailed reports on village finances are also prepared annually by the office of the Village Clerk, and the Treasurer, with other reports required to be filed with the State Comptroller and other State agencies. The State Comptroller's office makes examinations of the accounts and fiscal affairs of the village, which are submitted to the village Board.[46]

Village Budgets

Budget methods at the village level were redefined and modernized by state law in 1954. The entire budget process is spelled out in the village law and each village is provided by the state with a *Budget Manual for Villages,* prepared in considerable detail by the division of municipal affairs of the state comptroller's office. The local government officials also receive a manual on *Uniform System of Accounts for Villages.* These manuals are "prepared to assist officials of villages, and especially budget officers, in formulating a budget that will conform to proper accounting practices and legal requirement."[47]

[45] *Annual Report of the Incorporated Village of Garden City,* p. 12.

[46] *Ibid.,* p. 44.

[47] New York State Department of Audit and Control, *Budget Manual for Villages* (Albany), p. 1.

The village budget calendar is outlined in Table 11. The law requires the budget officer, in the person of the mayor or some one designated by him,[48] to initiate the preparation of the budget. He is also given the continuing responsibility to observe the budget in operation and report to the Board of Trustees. The budget officer is required to specify the form in which estimates are to be submitted.

TABLE 11

Village Budget Calendar [1]

	Fiscal Year Beginning:		
	June 1	**August 1**	**March 1**
A. Budget Officer notifies heads of administrative units in writing of the necessity for and form of estimates of revenues and expenses for the ensuing fiscal year §106(1) [1]	By February 8	By April 8	By November 8
B. Submission of estimates to Budget Officer §106(2)	By March 1	By May 1	By December 1
C. Preparation and filing of the tentative budget with the village clerk §107	By March 20	By May 20	By December 20
D. Review and preliminary alteration of tentative budget of Board of Trustees §109(1)	By March 31	By May 31	By December 31
E. Notice of public hearing on tentative budget; at least five days prior to hearing which shall be held not later than §109(3)	April 15	June 15	January 15
F. Public hearing; adjournments not later than §109(3)	April 20	June 20	January 20
G. Final revision of tentative budget	After public hearing but prior to adoption	After public hearing but prior to adoption	After public hearing but prior to adoption
H. Adoption of budget and appended salary and wage schedule §109(4)	By May 1	By July 1	By February 1

[1] Section references are to the village law.
Source: Budget Manual for Villages, p. 1.

In preparing the tentative budget, the budget officer "is not required to conform his recommendations of revenue or appropriations with those of the administrative units. If he concludes, as a

[48] Interview with village clerk, Garden City, April 1956. The budget officer for Garden City is the comptroller.

result of review or investigation, that an amount requested is either excessive or inadequate he may recommend appropriations of what he believes to be a necessary amount."[49] He must, however, file the estimated units with the village clerk at the time of the completion and filing of the tentative budget. The budget officer may prepare a budget message.

The tentative budget is presented to the Board of Trustees by the clerk of the board. The board can make such revisions as it wishes, provided:

a. that the statement of the estimate of the amount for any object or purpose for which an appropriation is required by law shall not be reduced below the minimum;

b. that all changes in the statement of estimate revenues be recorded in the minutes;

c. that the budget balance.

Following a public hearing, the village board may further change, alter, and review the budget.

Nassau's Two Cities

Glen Cove, situated on the North Shore, and Long Beach, located on the South Shore of Nassau, are smaller, both in population and area, than many of the villages in the county. Both of these cities are classified as third-class cities. Glen Cove has a Mayor Council form of government, while Long Beach has a Council Manager plan. Unlike the villages in the county, both Glen Cove and Long Beach have a representative sitting on the county Board of Supervisors. Both of these cities are beyond the jurisdiction of their respective town boards in the county.

D. THE SCHOOL DISTRICTS

Educating Nassau's children is the biggest governmental operation in Nassau County and there is no sign of any other function taking its place as the largest item of expense in the total county

[49] *Budget Manual for Villages,* p. 9.

governmental expenditures for a long time to come. The extraordinary population growth of Nassau and the high birth rate have levied and will continue to levy heavy demands upon the public schools. School districts are currently confronted with school enrollments in the thousands where a few years back they dealt with student bodies numbering in the hundreds. Districts whose school population ten years ago was roughly 10 per cent of their total population can soon expect to have between 20 and 25 per cent of their population enrolled in their public schools. At the present time, between 20 and 25 per cent of the population of Nassau, one quarter of a million, are in school. While the school population growth has been most dramatic, it has been very uneven. Newly built up areas such as Levittown have experienced an extraordinary increase in school enrollments and are now educating far more people than the older established school districts. "Returning to the instance of Levittown, its school enrollment in Union Free School District No. 5 increased from 35 pupils in 1948 to 19,226 in 1954, or nearly 300-fold in six years."[50] Contrast this with the situation in Garden City, Union Free School District No. 18, an established community where the increase in school enrollment from 1940 to 1955 was from 1799 pupils to 3546, or an increase just under 100 per cent in 15 years.[51]

Note the relative increase in the number of children under five years of age in 1940 and 1955 as opposed to the increase in the total school population in the same period. The problems inherent in this statistical breakdown are of course much greater and more complex in the many school districts whose school population has increased far more than 100 per cent. The per cent increase in the number of pupils in the entire county between 1950 and 1955 was 89.9 as opposed to 46.7 in Garden City.

The lack of uniformity, clearly evident in the rate of increase in school enrollment in different parts of Nassau County, is a characteristic of the education picture in Nassau County. The sixty-two school districts cover different size areas, ranging in acreage from 700 acres in Sea Cliff to 7,717 in Jericho. The percentage

50 Paul Studenski, "Fiscal Headaches for Metropolitan Areas," *GRA Reporter*, VII, No. 1 (1955), p. 11.

51 See Table 12.

TABLE 12

Population, Children, and School Enrollments in Garden City 1940, 1946, and 1950–1955

(a) U.S. Census Bureau.
(b) Estimated.
(c) LILCO estimate for January 1.
(d) School census taken November 15.

	Total Village Population	Children on Census Birth to 18 Years	Public School Enrollments K-6	Public School Enrollments 7-9	Public School Enrollments 10-12	Public School Enrollments Total	Private School Enroll-ment	Children under Five Years
1940	11,223 (a)	2,903	945	515	339	1799	349	430
1945	12,600 (b)	3,321	939	469	385	1793	441	713
1950	14,486 (a)	3,809	1282	480	528	2290	554	876
1951	15,280 (b)	4,349	1316	506	538	2360	769	1061
1952	16,154 (c)	4,715	1452	574	558	2584	818	1098
1953	17,140 (b)	5,159	1636	659	553	2848	892	1216
1954	18,228 (c)	5,726	1775	750	623	3148	1073	1330
1955	21,098 (d)	6,689	1942	883	721	3546	1227	1695

Source: Table prepared by Dr. William N. Leonard, Director of the Bureau of Research, Hofstra College, and presented as part of a talk at a School District meeting in May 1956.

of the land in each district used for residential, industrial, and other purposes also varies considerably from district to district. This use of land as residential, industrial, business, etc. is one of the key factors determining school population and tax burdens on the home owner. Dr. Studenski recently observed:

> To finance the huge expansion of their schools and other facilities, the suburbs have had but two main sources at their disposal—the property tax and state aid.
>
> In some instances, the suburbs contained substantial business and industry at the time the influx of the new population into them started, or else considerable business and industrial development took place in them soon thereafter. Such suburbs were able to obtain a considerable share of their needed additional funds from the taxation of business properties.
>
> But many suburbs have not been so fortunate. Being almost wholly residential from the outset and continuing to be so even with the new population, they have had to get the required additional funds almost entirely from the taxation of their new and old residents. Where their old residents were quite numerous and more prosperous than the new

ones, and also had fewer children of school age, it was they who had to bear a substantial share of the additional taxes required to supply schools and other municipal facilities to the newcomers. It must be noted that in suburbs composed wholly of home owners, the property tax operates very much like an income tax, each family contributing to the support of local government more or less in proportion to its income as reflected in the value of the home it owns. The proportionality is not as close as it can be under the income tax but there is a tendency in that direction.[52]

The figures in Table 13 on land use in Nassau County, while a few years out of date, indicate the general problem of the highly residential nature of the community and the obvious import of this situation where the chief source of revenue for school purposes is the property tax. The land use analyses presented here were prepared by the Nassau County Planning Commission on the basis of data obtained between 1950 and 1955.

TABLE 13

Nassau County Analyses

Analyses for Nassau County in its entirety and for the three towns follow. The percentages for the county are based upon a total area of 196,853 acres, or 307 square miles, and for the towns of Hempstead, North Hempstead, and Oyster Bay upon 89,336 acres, 33,151 acres, and 74,366 acres, respectively.

The water category includes both inland and off-shore water within the school district. As off-shore water was not included in the individual school district analyses, there is an increase of 14,125 acres of water over the individual school district's total.

Area in Acres	Per Cent of Total	Land Use	Area in Acres	Per Cent of Total
Nassau County			Town of Hempstead	
556	0.3	apartment	271	0.3
77,394	39.3	other residential	29,518	33.0
3,946	2.0	business	2,361	2.6
5,016	2.6	industrial	1,328	1.5
10,369	5.3	recreational	5,777	6.5
14,079	7.1	public	11,300	12.7
710	0.4	cemetery	392	0.4
47,208	24.0	vacant	15,648	17.5
18,982	9.6	street	10,128	11.3
2,822	1.4	parkway	1,760	2.0
15,771	8.0	water	10,853	12.2
196,853	100.0	TOTAL	89,336	100.0

52 Studenski, *loc. cit.*

TABLE 13 (*cont.*)

Area in Acres	Per Cent of Total	Land Use	Area in Acres	Per Cent of Total
Town of North Hempstead			Town of Oyster Bay	
247	0.7	apartment	38	0.1
17,324	52.3	other residential	30,552	41.1
610	1.8	business	975	1.3
1,916	5.8	industrial	1,772	2.4
1,415	4.3	recreational	3,177	4.3
1,148	3.4	public	1,631	2.2
156	0.5	cemetery	162	0.2
5,930	17.9	vacant	25,630	34.5
3,964	12.0	street	4,890	6.6
441	1.3	parkway	621	0.8
—	—	water	4,918	6.5
33,151	100.0	TOTAL	74,366	100.0

[1] Total Area for County. Two areas in the Town of Oyster Bay—namely—the Nassau County Sanitorium and the joint Oyster Bay-Babylon District comprising 97 and 703 acres, respectively, were not analyzed or included in the above area or percentage. Therefore, 800 acres must be added to this figure of 196,853 acres for a total area of Nassau County of 197,653 acres.

Source: Nassau County Planning Commission, **Planning Nassau County "Land Use,"** 1955.

The reader should notice the percentage figures indicating industrial and business land use. The figure for the county for both of these categories together is 4.6. For the towns of Hempstead, North Hempstead, and Oyster Bay the figures are 4.1, 7.6, and 3.7 respectively. Note also that at this time nearly a quarter of the land in Nassau was vacant. Even though this figure of 25 per cent has certainly been reduced considerably since this study was made, the need for intelligent planning and zoning of the area that is still vacant is imperative. Nassau does not have a strong, highly centralized planning program. Home rule provisions fragmenting the responsibility for planning and zoning do not help the situation, especially when these activities are usually engaged in by personnel limited in staff and funds, and hampered by a complex of governmental jurisdictions with authority to attempt to solve their own problems without necessarily considering the impact of their decisions on other agencies or units of government.

The League of Women Voters of one of the school districts in the county was quite impressed with this problem of land use and school taxes and undertook a study of the influence of commercial and industrial zoning on their school taxes. It is reproduced as Table 14. The figures speak for themselves.

TABLE 14

The Influence of Commercial and Industrial Zoning on the School Tax

Issued by the League of Women Voters of Oceanside, a non-partisan organization working to promote political responsibility through informed and active participation of citizens in government.

In a rapidly growing community such as ours there seems always to be considerable confusion as to the effect of new homes and new industries on our taxes. There are those who oppose incoming industry on the grounds that it has no place in a residential community, and there are others who believe that an increase in the number of homes will result in a decrease in the individual tax burden, and there are still others who believe that certain types of commercial and industrial enterprises will benefit the home owner taxwise. In the following table of assessments and taxes, the League hopes to clarify this issue as it relates to our school tax.

School Year 1954–1955
Tax Rate $3.50 Per $100 Assessed Value

Property	Zoning	Assessment	Average Children Per Home	Estimated Cost Per Pupil	Amount School Tax
1 Family Home	Res. "B"	$ 3,150	1.12	$319.47	$ 110.25
1 Family Home	Res. "B"	4,600	1.12	319.47	161.00
1 Family Home	Res. "B"	5,700	1.12	319.47	199.50
1 Family Home	Res. "B"	7,450	1.12	319.47	260.75
2 Story Bldg. Stores & Offices	Business	55,250	None	319.47	1,933.75
L. I. Water Co. Storage Tank	Business	81,410	None	319.47	2,849.35
Restaurant & Amusement Area	Business	86,450	None	319.47	3,025.75
Post Office	Business	24,000	None	319.47	840.00
Oil Company	Industrial	182,650	None	319.47	6,392.75
Manufacturing Co.	Industrial	27,500	None	319.47	962.50
Metal Co.	Industrial	63,800	None	319.47	2,233.00
Construction Co.	Industrial	31,850	None	319.47	1,114.75

From this table we see that a home would have to be assessed at approximately $10,223 at the current rate to pay the full cost of keeping 1.12 children in school for one year. Since very few homes in our school district carry so high an assessment, it is obvious that commercial and industrial properties, which have no children to educate, contribute the difference. It is further seen that the building of homes increases the school tax rate, while the arrival of commercial and industrial properties lowers it.

EXPLANATION OF TABLES

1. *Zoning:* The zoning of Oceanside is established by the town of Hempstead. Zoning classifications include Residence "A," "B," "C," "C-A," Light Manufacturing and Industry. Oceanside has no Residence "A" or "C-A." To better understand the zoning classifications, a booklet called *Building Zone Ordinance,* issued by the Town of Hempstead, may be purchased for 50¢ at the Town Hall. A copy may be examined at the Oceanside Library.

2. *Assessment:* Assessed valuation of property is established by the County Board of Assessors for all of Nassau County. Assessment rolls are open to all citizens. The third Tuesday in May is known as "Grievance Day." The taxpayer who believes his property unfairly assessed may ask for a review before the Board.

3. *Average Children Per Home:* 1.12 is the last figure obtained in a 1951–52 professional survey made of the school district. The increase in population has been predominately young couples with pre-school children, the impact of which will not be felt in our school enrollment for several years.

4. *Estimated Cost Per Pupil:* This figure is based on the estimated average daily attendance for the current school year. The total cost per pupil on the total budget of $2,563,077 is *$473.24*. However, state aid in the amount of $832,854.22 reduced the net budget to be raised by school district taxation to $1,730,222.78. This means that the cost per pupil to be sustained by the local taxpayer is $319.47.

GENERAL INFORMATION

Union Free School District No. 11
(Oceanside School District)

Area: Includes all of Oceanside and a small section of Rockville Centre and Baldwin

Assessed Valuation: $46,635,550

Schools: 6 Elementary, 1 Junior High, 1 Senior High School (to be opened in the fall)

1955–56 School Enrollment: 6,600 (estimated)

The superintendent's annual report to the Board of Education, a highly informative booklet, may be had at the administrative office in the junior high school.

In order graphically to present a true picture, the League made a zoning map of Oceanside. This map indicates in color the zoning classifications and *permitted* land-use in our area. A large scale copy has been made for the Oceanside Planning Committee for the use of Civic Associations, one has been offered to the Oceanside Board of Trade, another, smaller in scale, is on view at the Oceanside Library.

In the making is a more detailed series of maps showing *actual* land-use. When completed, these will identify all existing buildings, stores, apartments, service stations, tax free properties, etc. As a by-product of these maps, the League has compiled an extensive list of goods and services in our community.

The lack of uniformity in Nassau's school organization is further evidenced in the various tax rates (discussed in the section on revenue), teachers' salaries, amounts of state aid received by each district, and the amounts of money spent per pupil on the basis of average daily attendance.

The average daily attendance and the cost per pupil for the county school districts for the fiscal year 1954–1955 is shown in Table 15.

TABLE 15

Average Daily Attendance and Amount Spent Per Capita [1]

Average Daily Attendance	Amount Spent Per Capita	Average Daily Attendance	Amount Spent Per Capita
10	511.90	2788	445.64
106	918.87	2804	270.78
148	719.19	2854	545.51
220	512.18	2955	512.16
278	602.55	2986	419.84
418	511.12	2989	396.59
629	358.70	3038	423.88
655	559.91	3203	523.06
776	755.06	3282	324.35
1174	509.30	3307	307.96
1301	409.55	3380	481.34
1312	701.86	3456	541.71
1339	1062.41	3511	369.84
1404	505.27	3521	495.69
1441	728.26	3632	478.29
1616	434.34	4088	449.58
1732	552.67	4259	486.50
1798	365.85	4415	415.54
1847	376.29	4463	497.90
1874	303.33	4579	377.41
2025	345.47	4810	507.11
2069	469.16	4883	399.49
2151	528.92	5114	548.52
2213	760.15	5405	364.87
2265	691.15	6295	338.30
2458	409.78	6778	500.71
2459	510.12	7440	617.89
2497	635.82	7456	319.23
2541	453.73	9074	298.13
2579	368.36	10729	344.68
2727	314.88		

[1] The figures represent the average daily attendance and cost per pupil based on total current expenses less special schools divided by total average daily attendance.

Source: Data provided the author by the New York State Department of Education.

The Administration of Nassau County's School System

The marked lack of uniformity indicated above in many aspects of education in the county is essentially a reflection of the fact that unlike the centralized school system of New York, which serves a million children, Nassau County has sixty-two separate and distinct school systems. Each district is administered by a locally elected school board.

The school districts in Nassau County fall into one of three categories—common school districts, central school districts, and union free school districts—each with the power to levy property taxes for schools.

Common school districts are permitted to provide for education at the elementary school level only. Union free and central school districts provide education through the twelfth year. The central school district represents a combination of common, union free, or city school districts.

The overwhelming majority of school districts in Nassau are union free school districts, two central school districts, three central high school districts and fifty-three union free school districts providing educational services in the county. If the union free or central school district chooses to hire a superintendent of schools, the office is referred to as a "village" superintendency. This does not mean that the boundaries of these particular districts are coterminous with those of a particular incorporated village; they are not. In fact, some of the newer "village" superintendencies such as Levittown and East Meadow are in the heart of the unincorporated area of Nassau.

There are 28 "village" superintendent school districts in Nassau County. The other 34 of the county's school districts are assigned on the basis of their township location, to one of the supervisory districts in the county.

Nassau County maintains two Supervisory Districts to assist school districts not having their own superintendent. The district supervisors aid in the overall planning of new buildings, problems of financing, and the development of the study curriculum necessary to meet the educational needs of 34 of the county's school districts. Village school districts with their own superintendent, including some of the larger incorporated villages, do not come under this jurisdiction. The First Supervisory District includes the towns of North Hempstead and Oyster Bay. The Second Supervisory District, the largest such district in the United States, embraces the town of Hempstead.[53]

The State Education Law provides that the number of members of the Board of Education of a union free school district shall not be fewer than three or more than nine. This elected board runs the school system of the district. It prepares the annual budget, hires teachers, contracts for purchases, provides bus transportation, etc. Many of its decisions are subject to the support of the voters of the district.

The five-member board in the Garden City school district, for example, elects its chairman or president. The board members are unsalaried laymen who give extraordinary time and effort to their task of running the school system of their community. Like many other school districts, this board of District 18 depends heavily upon its staff, the superintendent, and the assistant superintendent for business in particular, in the general management and fiscal affairs of the district.

The preparation of the budget for the Garden City school system begins in December when the call for estimates goes out under the superintendent's name. The estimates are returnable by February first to the office of the assistant superintendent for business. The members of the board and its staff review these various estimates in what might be called executive budget hearings. Following its active participation in the preparation of the budget, the board adopts the budget in April and submits it to the voters in the district in early May.

The Garden City district, like many other school districts in Nassau, had to reevaluate its administrative organization in light of the constantly increasing enrollment and the demands it makes upon the school system. As school budgets rise into the millions, school taxes double every few years, and school buildings spring up in every direction, the need for expert staff assistance to the school boards and their superintendents becomes more than obvious.

[53] Nassau County, *Your County Nassau* (Mineola, 1955).

The Garden City Board of Education has shown that it is cognizant of the problem of providing managerial assistance to the people responsible for administering the schools by its recent action in having the center for community and field services of the NYU School of Education make a study of its school system. The report of this study group in 1955 called attention to the need to strengthen the hand of the superintendent in administrative as well as educational aspects of the whole school setup. The recommendations that the assistant superintendent for business management be responsible not only for budget and finance, but for pupil transportation, maintenance and operation of school plants, and supervision of central office personnel who take care of budget and accounts, purchasing and secretarial services, as well, have been endorsed and adopted. Other school districts have taken similar steps. While the trend seems to be to provide the local school administrations with business managers, is this enough? Can school budgets running well over one and two million dollars each be adequately prepared and administered by business managers, who are so overtaxed with today's problems that they have little time for further planning, cost analysis, management surveys, or comparative studies of the operating efficiency of similar parts of the whole system or the efficiency of one school system as compared to that of another district? Here once again, as in other governmental functions in the county, Nassau's twin problems of fragmented responsibility and inadequate provisions for effective management of these functions stand out. These problems are not new; they are just much more acute than they were, and they are beginning to receive considerably more public attention.

The author of one report on Nassau as far back as twenty-two years ago commented, in discussing Nassau's even more semi-rural governmental setup than we know today, as follows:

> There is no function of government in Nassau County which cries more loudly for unification under strong central control than education. . . . Nassau County children do not have equal educational opportunities, nor do Nassau County taxpayers bear equal burdens for school support. Very much the contrary is true. The general cost of education too is higher than it needs to be if supplied by a single well organized department. The cost of administration as contrasted with in-

struction and other elements in school expenditures is high—largely because there are too many units with administrative overhead. Salaries are on the whole high, but with wide variations from district to district. Even the "cuts" of 1934 leave the school budgets still high. This is a situation which can be corrected only by salary standardization on a reasonable scale at the hands of a central county authority.

And yet, strong as are the arguments for unified school administration, we hesitate to recommend consolidation at this time. The very extremes of diversity which mark the present educational setup in the county indicate a degree of "localism" as far as schools are concerned far in excess of that which supports independent police and fire departments. In this respect, Nassau County does not differ from other communities in our country. Everywhere, the people show more interest and more local pride in their schools than in any other institution of government, often several times over.[54]

The school issues raised in this report of 1934 are still basically the issues Nassau and its residents are faced with today. In 1955 Robert Moses told a planning forum on the problems of growth in Nassau and western Suffolk:

A word finally about schools—your greatest problem. In Nassau today there is a hodge-podge of little red and big modern school houses populated by pupils some of whom are studying Mutt and Jeff, Hopalong Cassidy, and Davy Crockett, while others are becoming proficient in quaternions, nuclear science, and the Venerable Bede. Members of school boards are almost as numerous as members of the French Legion of Honor, the Elks and the Christmas Clubs.

He continued:

You have in my opinion too many districts of widely varying sizes and efficiency. Some are poor, others are not. The rates are scandalously unequal. I see no ultimate solution but a County School Budget Board, preparing estimates for the entire county, collecting one county-wide tax and distributing the receipts to local districts which should be gradually consolidated still leaving administrative local autonomy. This will promote uniformly high standards but still preserve home rule.[55]

Mr. Moses and many others are joined in their feeling that

[54] Municipal Consultant Service of the National Municipal League, *op. cit.*, pp. 56–57.

[55] Robert Moses, "The Future of Nassau and Western Suffolk: Introductory Remarks," *The Probems of Growth in Nassau and Western Suffolk,* Hempstead, 1955, p. 6.

something must be done about Nassau's educational system. The widespread agreement on the need for action is matched by the widespread disagreement on just what form the action should take. A recent article "Crisis in Our Schools" appearing in *Newsday* included in its summary the following list of possible alternative courses of action:

1. A higher state income tax to finance a greater proportion of school costs from state aid. This is suggested by Nicholas B. Englehardt, Jr., nationally-known expert in school finance, among others.

Under such a plan, Long Islanders would pay higher income taxes but the owner of the $14,000 home would pay much less in proportion than if the major burden was left on local real estate.

The argument for it is that it taps wealth which the property tax cannot reach and tends to equalize financial resources of areas with industry and those with little or none.

2. More federal aid to education. At present some school districts near defense installations or plants get help from Washington. A bill now before Congress would put U. S. credit behind school bonds but would only give a trickle of direct aid.

There are serious objections to federal aid by those who feel that federal control would come right along with the aid. The objection to state aid on such grounds is not so serious—the state already has a good deal of control of the schools which are chartered under the state.

3. Centralization. This is the solution that the state would like to see more Long Island districts adopt. By centralizing several small districts into one large district, schools would get more state aid and have a broader tax base. The state hopes that many Long Island districts, particularly in Suffolk, will centralize but acknowledges that Long Island's growth is so rapid that a district small enough to centralize this year may be big enough for a school program of its own within a few years.

4. Pooling of all non-residential school taxes in each county to be returned to local districts under some formula similar to the one now used by Albany for state aid. This would eliminate some inequities which now exist between school districts, particularly the obvious inequity of a large business or industry which receives revenues from all parts of the county but pays school taxes to only one district.

5. A further extension of 4-county-wide taxing of all real estate for school purposes, each district to get its share on a school population basis. This is the plan suggested by Park Commissioner Moses. It has the same objections as the fourth proposal—the wealthy communities kick at sharing with their less wealthy neighbors.

6. New kinds of taxes. Counties, under a 1951 law, can impose a sales tax. A one per cent sales tax would bring in between $7,000,000 and

$8,000,000, in Nassau alone. Counties can also impose liquor taxes and taxes on admissions, as well as utilities taxes on consumers. However, counties cannot tax admissions to race tracks. An odd clause in the state law allows only cities with populations of more than 125,000 to tax admissions to race tracks and oddly enough New York City is the only one to qualify.[56]

[56] J. Blackney, "Crisis in Our Schools," *Newsday*, October 26, 1955, p. 7c. This is the fifth article of a series of five on the particular subject.

Part II
Expenditures and Revenues

A. THE PATTERN OF GOVERNMENTAL EXPENDITURES IN NASSAU COUNTY

The trend of expenditures in Nassau County since World War II has been constantly upward. A recent study of fiscal affairs in New York State considers the factors behind the great increase in governmental expenditures at the local level not only in Nassau but throughout the state.

> During World War II, the operating costs of local government were comparatively stable, largely because of factors such as deferred plant and equipment maintenance, non-replacement of employees in the armed forces and a decline in welfare costs and school enrollment—most of which were not only temporary but were sure to have an explosive effect on costs after the war. Other well-known factors have contributed to the postwar upward trend, such as the rising price level, accelerated growth and shifting population, increase in school enrollment, the backlog of capital improvements, and the demand for more and better services by a more affluent population.[1]

Today, Nassau's governments spend over a quarter of a billion dollars annually. In 1954 the figure was $264,817,014.33.[2] This represents an increase over the 1945 figure, $49,085,402.46,[3] of 439 per cent. Consideration of Table 18 shows clearly the pronounced upward trend.

While current expenditures increased 307 per cent, total expenditures including capital outlay rose much more sharply. In 1945 expenditures for capital outlay were $1,534,457.74, or roughly 8.5 million dollars less than those for debt service principal. In 1954 expenditures for capital outlay ($75,150,162.60) represented about twice the amount spent for debt service.

1 Temporary Commission on the Fiscal Affairs of State Government, *A Program For Continued Progress In Fiscal Management,* I (1955), 122.

2 See Table 16.

3 See Table 19; see also Appendix D.

TABLE 16

Expenditures [1] by Function for Nassau County and All Units Located Therein—Fiscal Years Ending in 1954

Current Expenditures	Total	County	Cities	Towns	Special Districts	Villages	School Districts	Fire Districts
General Government	$ 13,177,135.60	$ 7,455,914.28	$ 544,924.91	$ 2,678,980.84	$	$ 2,497,315.57	$	$
Protection Persons & Prop.	15,023,207.84	8,488,821.95	722,301.70	299,844.53	323,806.47	3,858,288.92		1,330,144.27
Health	2,456,502.40	2,399,736.79	19,500.00	13,945.88		23,319.73		
Sanitation	8,494,641.67	963,878.30	473,668.91	661,772.99	3,628,320.41	2,767,001.06		
Highways	11,330,853.55	3,030,763.22	442,648.95	4,886,350.60		2,971,090.78		
Education	67,048,523.87	48,433.77		5,972.85			66,994,117.25	
Welfare Administration	1,276,355.88	1,273,656.60	1,199.28	1,500.00				
Old Age Assistance	1,732,756.75	1,732,756.75						
Aid to Dependent Children	729,482.05	729,482.05						
Aid to Blind	53,471.87	53,471.87						
Home Relief	226,138.32	226,138.32						
Hospital Care	101,175.24	101,175.24						
Burials	14,954.73	14,954.73						
Aid to Disabled	487,465.21	487,465.21						
Foster Care	667,060.15	667,060.15						
Adult Institutional Care	20,751.57	20,751.57						
Other Assistance	290,068.92	290,068.92						
Correction	380,390.43	380,390.43						
Libraries & Museums	298,173.88		18,548.81			279,625.07		
Recreation	2,623,489.36	1,128,577.46	301,572.59	495,730.49		697,608.82		
Hospitals	6,250,736.15	6,250,736.15						
Natural Resources	26,988.89	26,988.89						
All Other	6,461,404.11	5,495,349.86	104,437.46	61,076.43	796,087.80	4,452.56		
Special Activities	360,359.01	272,660.72	79,884.75	7,813.54				
Water Maintenance	2,280,338.98		148,259.62		1,179,886.00	952,193.36		
Light Maintenance	2,942,905.22				1,104,933.25	1,837,971.97		
Debt Service: Interest	8,102,299.66	2,660,591.20	265,189.47	208,316.68	482,108.79	489,743.07	3,929,704.87	66,645.58
Total All Current Expend.	$152,857,631.31	$44,199,824.43	$3,122,136.45	9,321,304.83	$ 7,515,142.72	$16,378,610.91	$ 70,923,822.12	$1,396,789.85
Capital Outlay	75,150,162.60	22,627,205.91	876,206.98	2,417,571.44	2,918,956.38	5,092,430.56	40,735,941.40	481,849.93
Total Current & Capital	$228,007,793.91	$66,827,030.34	$3,998,343.43	$11,738,876.27	$10,434,099.10	$21,471,041.47	$111,659,763.52	$1,878,639.78
Debt Service: Principal	36,809,220.42	12,843,750.00	860,316.67	902,250.00	2,750,772.04	7,658,219.21	11,400,136.75	393,775.75
Total All Expenditures	$264,817,014.33	$79,670,780.34	$4,858,660.10	$12,641,126.27	$13,184,871.14	$29,129,260.68	$123,059,900.29	$2,272,415.53

[1] Does not include transfers, trust and investment transactions.

Source: Figures derived from New York State Comptroller, **Special Report on Municipal Affairs,** Legislative Document (1955) No. 33A (Albany: Fort Orange Press, 1955) and tabulations made by the Research and Statistics Section of the Division of Municipal Affairs of the New York State Department of Audit and Control, in November 1955, from annual reports filed in the comptroller's office.

TABLE 17

Expenditures [1] by Function for Nassau County and All Units Located Therein—Fiscal Years Ending in 1945

Current Expenditures	Total	County	Cities	Towns	Special Districts	Villages	School Districts	Fire Districts
General Government	$ 4,158,895.86	$ 2,406,150.31	$ 251,055.53	$ 673,339.95	$	$ 828,350.07	$	$
Protection Persons & Property	4,255,252.72	2,089,283.23	327,888.66	64,316.27	81,187.67	1,377,477.62		815,099.27
Health	1,406,756.86	1,373,334.31	28.10	25,075.30		8,319.15		
Sanitation	2,125,705.98	177,382.93	242,742.97		685,195.03	1,020,385.05		
Highways	3,797,104.45	1,650,148.46	200,508.96	895,894.08		1,050,552.95		
Education	14,052,825.62	89,825.68	813,940.77	2,080.00			13,146,979.17	
Welfare Administration	416,190.53	416,190.53						
Old Age Assistance	828,779.72	828,779.72						
Aid to Dependent Children	336,780.84	336,780.84						
Aid to Blind	12,985.78	12,985.78						
Home Relief	263,833.98	263,833.98						
Veterans	11,181.80	10,781.80	400.00					
Other Assistance	615,594.47	610,594.47	5,000.00					
Correction	191,084.30	191,084.30						
Libraries & Museums	78,097.79		11,848.44			66,249.35		
Recreation	560,489.89	122,587.06	131,671.16	127,788.34		178,443.33		
All Other Current	314,745.97		93,514.01	5,501.52	158,368.70	57,361.74		
Water Maintenance	632,299.02		103,201.02		170,950.18	358,147.82		
Light Maintenance	1,056,320.89				417,538.73	638,782.16		
Debt Service: Interest	2,416,283.05	1,344,890.87	383,083.20	15,619.09	198,222.05	470,199.59		4,268.25
Total All Current Expenditures	$37,531,209.52	$11,924,634.27	$2,564,882.82	$1,809,614.55	$1,711,462.36	$6,054,268.83	$13,146,979.17	$319,367.52
Capital Outlay	1,534,457.74	350,546.29	188,559.65	307,992.91	8,294.21	295,897.27	273,940.46	109,226.95
Total Current & Capital	$39,065,667.26	$12,275,180.56	$2,753,442.47	$2,117,607.46	$1,719,756.57	$6,350,166.10	$13,420,919.63	$428,594.47
Debt Service: Principal	10,019,735.20	3,420,000.00	768,213.23	28,000.00	694,967.00	2,269,641.89	2,804,633.08	34,280.00
Total All Expenditures	$49,085,402.46	$15,695,180.56	$3,521,655.70	$2,145,607.46	$2,414,723.57	$8,619,807.99	$16,225,552.71	$462,874.47

[1] Does not include transfers, trust and investment transactions.

Source: Figures derived from New York State Comptroller, **Special Report on Municipal Affairs,** Legislative Document (1946) No. 70 (Albany: Fort Orange Press, 1946).

TABLE 18

Local Government Expenditures in Nassau County, 1945 and 1954[1]

	1945	1954	Increase	Per Cent of Increase
Total Expenditures	49,085,402.46	264,817,014.33	215,731,611.87	439
Current Expenditures[2]	37,531,209.52	152,857,631.31	115,326,421.79	307
Capital Outlay	1,534,457.74	75,150,162.60	73,615,704.86	4797
Debt Service Principal	10,019,735.20	36,809,220.42	26,789,485.22	267

[1] For fiscal years ending in 1945 and 1954.
[2] Includes interest on the debt.

No matter how the figures of the local government expenditures in Nassau are examined, one cannot help but be aware of the great rise in governmental costs and the pronounced shifts in the pattern of expenditures since 1945.

Distribution of Expenditures by Classes of Government

Nassau county's school districts spend nearly half of all the money spent in the county by the local units of government. In 1954, the local school boards spent $123,059,900.29 or 48.97 per cent of the total expenditures the units of government in Nassau reported for the fiscal years ending in 1954, while in 1945 the school expenditures involved 34.34 per cent of the total spent.

Excluding payments on the principal of debts and outlays for permanent improvements, we find that the expenditures by classes of government were as follows:

	1945	1954
County	$11,924,634.27	$44,199,824.43
Cities	2,564,882.82	3,122,136.45
Towns	1,809,614.55	9,321,304.83
Villages	6,054,268.83	16,378,610.91
School District	13,146,979.17	70,923,822.12
Fire District	319,367.52	1,396,789.85
Other District	1,711,462.36	7,515,142.72
Total cost of government	$37,531,209.52	$152,857,631.31

In 1945 expenditures for current items by the various units of government were such that 35.02 per cent of the total was expended by the numerous school boards, 31.71 per cent by the county government, 16.13 per cent by the villages, 6.83 per cent by the cities, 4.82 per cent by the towns, 4.56 per cent by the special districts and .86 per cent by the fire districts. The 1954 pattern was quite different. The school boards still spent the largest part of the total but it had risen to 46.40 per cent. The county dropped to 28.91 per cent of the total, the village fell to 10.71 per cent of the total, but the towns and special districts increased to 6.10 per cent and 4.92 per cent respectively. The cities fell to 2.04 per cent of the total, and the fire districts rose slightly to .91 per cent. (Figures do not total 100 per cent because of rounding.)

TABLE 19

Percentage Distribution [1] of Expenditures for Governmental Services by Units of Government in Nassau County for the Fiscal Years Ending in 1945

Current Expenditures	Total	County	Cities	Towns	Special Dists.	Villages	School Dists.	Fire Dists.
General Government	100	57.85	6.04	16.19		19.92		
Protection, Persons & Prop.	100	49.09	7.71	1.51	1.91	32.37		7.41
Health	100	97.62	.006	1.78		.60		
Sanitation	100	8.34	11.42		32.23	48.01		
Highways	100	43.45	5.29	23.59		27.67		
Education	100	.63	5.80	.01			93.56	
Welfare Administration	100	100.00						
Old Age Assistance	100	100.00						
Aid to Dependent Children	100	100.00						
Aid to Blind	100	100.00						
Home Relief	100	100.00						
Veterans	100	96.42	3.58					
Other Assistance	100	99.18	.82					
Correction	100	100.00						
Libraries and Museums	100		15.17			84.33		
Recreation	100	21.87	23.49	22.80		31.84		
All Other	100		29.71	1.74	50.32	18.23		
Water Maintenance	100		16.32		27.03	56.65		
Light Maintenance	100				39.52	60.48		
Debt Service: Interest	100	55.66	15.85	.65	8.20	19.46		.18
Total All Current Expenditures	100	31.71	6.83	4.82	4.56	16.13	35.02	.86
Capital Outlay	100	22.84	12.29	20.07	.54	19.28	17.86	7.12
Total Current & Capital	100	31.41	7.05	5.41	4.41	16.25	34.34	1.10

[1] Figures may not add to 100 per cent because of rounding source. See Table 17.

The shifting pattern of expenditures reflecting the increase of school enrollment and the tremendous growth of population in the unincorporated areas served by the town and special districts is further emphasized by a review of the rate of increase in current expenditures from 1945 to 1954 among the different classes of local government. The rates in descending scale were: school districts, 439 per cent; towns, 415 per cent; special districts, 339 per cent; fire districts, 337 per cent; county, 270 per cent; villages, 170 per cent; and cities, 21 per cent.

Before we turn our attention to the question of what the money is spent for rather than who is spending it, a brief glance at the rate of increase in total expenditures from 1945 to 1954 among the different classes of local government might prove significant. The rates, also in descending order, were: school districts, 657 per cent; towns, 489 per cent; special districts, 446 per cent; county, 407 per cent; fire district, 390 per cent; villages, 237 per cent; and cities, 37 per cent.

What Is the Money Spent For?

Nassau's governments reported that roughly one-third of their funds[4] were spent for capital outlay for the fiscal years ending in 1954. This heavy investment in the construction, improvement, and acquisition of fixed assets for the immediate and distant needs of the county community clearly indicates the obvious sequel, higher budgets for current expenses in future years. Schools mean more teachers, hospitals mean more staff, new buildings must be maintained, and wider roads require upkeep and policing.

The reader should note that of the 75 million dollars spent for capital purposes out of a total capital-current expenditure of 228 million, 54 per cent or nearly 41 million dollars was spent for schools by the county's school boards. The county government spent another 30 per cent of the total used for capital purposes in 1954. (See Table 20.)

[4] This figure is based on total capital and current expenditures and does not include payments for debt retirement.

TABLE 20

Percentage Distribution[1] of Expenditures for Governmental Services by Units of Government in Nassau County for the Fiscal Years Ending in 1954

Current Expenditures	Total	County	Cities	Towns	Special Dists.	Villages	School Dists.	Fire Dists.
General Government	100	56.57	4.13	20.33		18.97		
Protection, Persons & Prop.	100	56.50	4.81	2.00	2.15	25.68		8.86
Health	100	97.68	.80	.57		.95		
Sanitation	100	11.34	5.58	7.79	42.71	32.58		
Highways	100	26.75	3.90	43.13		26.22		
Education	100	.07		.01			99.89	
Welfare Administration	100	99.78	.10	.12				
Old Age Assistance	100	100.00						
Aid to Dependent Children	100	100.00						
Aid to Blind	100	100.00						
Home Relief	100	100.00						
Hospital Care	100	100.00						
Burials	100	100.00						
Aid to Disabled	100	100.00						
Foster Care	100	100.00						
Adult Institutional Care	100	100.00						
Other Assistance	100	100.00						
Correction	100	100.00						
Libraries & Museums	100		6.22			93.78		
Recreation	100	43.01	11.50	18.89		26.60		
Hospital	100	100.00						
Natural Resources	100	100.00						
All Other	100	85.04	1.62	.95	12.32	.07		
Special Activities	100	77.84	22.66					
Water Maintenance	100		6.50		51.74	41.76		
Light Maintenance	100				37.54	62.46		
Debt Service: Interest	100	32.83	3.28	2.57	5.95	6.04	48.50	.83
Total All Current Expenditures	100	28.91	2.04	6.10	4.92	10.71	46.40	.91
Capital Outlay	100	30.09	1.16	3.22	3.88	6.78	54.17	.65
Total Current & Capital	100	29.30	1.76	5.15	4.57	9.42	48.97	.82

[1] Figures may not add to 100 per cent because of rounding source. See Table 16.

The second largest amount of the total sum spent by Nassau County and all its subdivisions was for education. Twenty-nine per cent or 67 million dollars of the total of 228 million was to run the educational plants. This figure represents 46 per cent of all the money spent in Nassau for current expenses in that year. Of this money 99.9 per cent was spent by the local boards of education.

Next to education the most important governmental function appears to be the protection of persons and property. The governments of Nassau spent roughly 6.6 per cent of their total current and capital expenditures or about 10 per cent of their total current expenditures for police and fire protection. The sum of 15 million dollars was spent in the following way: the county accounted for 56.5 per cent of the total; the two cities 4.81 per cent, the towns 2.0 per cent; the special districts 2.15 per cent; the villages 25.68 per cent, and the fire districts 8.86 per cent. Here one sees the wide dispersion of responsibility for providing police and fire protection to the residents of Nassau.

General government, which covers the cost of compensation of officials in the executive, legislative, and judicial branches of local government, amounted to just over 13 million dollars or 5.77 per cent of the total. Maintenance of roads, snow removal compensations, and expenses of office of street commissioners cost nearly 4 million or 4.97 per cent of the total. As in other governmental functions, several different units of government spent parts of the amount involved in highway operation. Forty-three per cent was spent by the towns; just over 25 per cent by the county; slightly less than the county by the villages, and about 4 per cent by the two cities.

The governments of Nassau spent the following percentages of the total for their additional activities: 3.7 for sanitation, 3.56 for interest on the debt, 2.74 for hospitals, 2.64 for welfare, and 1.08 for health. Less than 1.5 per cent of the money spent in 1954 was for recreation and libraries combined.

In sharp contrast to the 1954 pattern of expenditures, the situation in 1945 was such that less than 4 per cent of the reported local governmental expenditures was for capital improvements. In 1954 capital outlay accounted for one-third of the amount spent for operating expenses and capital expenditures.

Other shifts in the expenditures by function since 1945 are for the most part downward relative to the total expenditures for current and capital purposes. Current expenses for education were 35.97 per cent of the total in 1945 and in 1954 were about 30 per cent of the total. Protection of persons and property took 11 per cent in 1945 and in 1954 accounted for about 7 per cent. General government expenditures dropped from over 10 per cent to under 6 per cent. Highways accounted for more than 9 per cent in 1945 and in 1954 took less than 5 per cent of the total.

The pattern of expenditures in 1945 is presented in Table 22; that for 1954 in Table 21.

There has also been a shift in the relative amount spent by the various classes of government in providing these services and func-

TABLE 21

Percentage Distribution[1] of Expenditures by Function for Nassau County and All Units Located Therein for Fiscal Years Ending in 1954

Current Expenditures	Total	County	Cities	Towns	Special Dists.	Villages	School Dists.	Fire Dists.
General Government	5.77	11.15	13.63	22.82		11.63		
Protection, Persons & Prop.	6.59	12.70	18.06	2.56	3.10	17.97		70.80
Health	1.08	3.59	.49	.12		.11		
Sanitation	3.73	1.45	11.84	5.63	34.77	12.89		
Highways	4.97	4.53	11.07	41.62		13.83		
Education	29.40	.07		.06			59.99	
Welfare Administration	.56	1.91	.03	.01				
Old Age Assistance	.76	2.59						
Aid to Dependent Children	.32	1.09						
Aid to Blind	.03	.08						
Home Relief	.09	.34						
Hospital Care	.05	.15						
Burials	.01	.02						
Aid to Disabled	.21	.73						
Foster Care	.29	1.00						
Adult Institutional Care	.01	0.3						
Other Assistance	.13	.44						
Correction	.16	.56						
Libraries & Museums	.14		.47			1.31		
Recreation	1.15	1.69	7.54	4.22		3.24		
Hospitals	2.74	9.35						
Natural Resources	.01	.04						
All Other	2.83	8.23	2.61	.52	7.63	0.3		
Special Activities	.16	.40	2.00	.07				
Water Maintenance	1.00		3.71		11.30	4.43		
Light Maintenance	1.29				10.59	8.56		
Debt Service: Interest	3.56	3.98	6.63	1.77	4.62	2.28	3.53	3.55
Total All Current Expenditures	67.02	66.12	78.08	79.40	72.01	76.28	63.52	74.35
Capital Outlay	32.86	33.85	21.92	20.60	27.98	23.72	36.48	25.65
Total Current and Capital	100.00	100.00	100.00	100.00	100.00	100.00	100.00	100.00

[1] Figures may not add to 100 per cent because of rounding source. See Table 16.

TABLE 22

Percentage Distribution[1] of Expenditures by Function for Nassau County and All Units Located Therein for Fiscal Years Ending in 1945

Current Expenditures	Total	County	Cities	Towns	Special Dists.	Villages	School Dists.	Fire Dists.
General Government	10.64	19.60	9.11	31.79		13.04		
Protection, Persons & Prop.	10.89	17.02	11.91	3.04	4.74	21.69		73.52
Health	3.60	11.19	.007	1.18		.14		
Sanitation	5.44	1.44	8.82		40.08	16.08		
Highways	9.71	13.45	7.28	42.31		16.55		
Education	35.97	.73	29.56	.10			97.95	
Welfare Administration	1.06	3.39						
Old Age Assistance	2.12	6.75						
Aid to Dependent Children	.86	2.74						
Aid to Blind	.04	.11						
Home Relief	.67	2.15						
Veterans	.03	.08	.02					
Other Assistance	1.58	4.98	.18					
Correction	.48	1.56						
Libraries & Museums	.20		.43			1.04		
Recreation	1.44	.99	4.78	6.03		2.81		
All Other Current	.80		3.40	.26	9.26	.90		
Water Maintenance	1.62		3.74		10.00	5.64		
Light Maintenance	2.71				24.42	10.06		
Debt Service: Interest	6.18	10.96	13.92	.74	11.59	7.41	—	.99
Total All Current Expenditures	96.04	97.14	93.15	85.45	100.09	95.36	97.95	74.51
Capital Outlay	3.93	2.86	6.85	14.55	.49	4.66	2.05	25.49
Total Current and Capital	100.00	100.00	100.00	100.00	100.00	100.00	100.00	100.00

[1] Figures may not add to 100 per cent because of rounding source. See Table 17.

tions for Nassau's residents. In 1954 and 1945 the percentage distribution of the total money spent in the county by local units for public safety was as follows:

	1954	1945
The County	56.50%	49.09%
The Cities	7.18%	7.71%
The Towns	2.00%	1.51%
The Special Districts	2.15%	1.91%
The Villages	25.68%	32.37%
The Fire Districts	8.86%	7.41%

The differences in the expenditure pattern by class of government for highways were these:

	1954	1945
The County	26.75%	43.45%
The Cities	3.90%	5.29%
The Towns	43.13%	23.59%
The Villages	26.22%	27.67%

The differences in the expenditure pattern by class of government for sanitation were as follows:

	1954	1945
The County	11.34%	8.34%
The Cities	5.58%	11.42%
The Towns	7.79%	
The Special Districts	42.71%	32.33%
The Villages	32.58%	48.01%

In each of the above instances the incorporated areas, the cities and villages, are found to be playing a less significant role in providing these governmental services to the residents of the county. On the other hand, the towns and the special districts are clearly playing a larger role in the total scheme of things in Nassau. These data once again indicate the great expansion and growth of the unincorporated areas of the county. It is interesting to note that the increased role of the county in public safety can be traced in large measure to the fact that the unincorporated areas get their police protection from the county through a police district device.

In the following pages, the author tries to present a breakdown of the expenditure pattern of each of the various classes of government whose expenditures have just been reviewed in terms of the grand total spent by all the local units of government in the county. The writer also attempts to indicate, through the use of budget figures for the fiscal years ending in 1956, that the general pattern of governmental spending in Nassau in 1954 was continued into 1956.

Governments are spending more each year. Capital expenditures are still a large item in the total picture. School expenditures continue to dominate the pattern. The governments providing services to the residents of the unincorporated areas of the county are still spending an increasingly larger share of total expenditures for governmental activities in Nassau.

The County Government's Expenditures

With respect to the amount of money spent for operating expenses, in 1954 protection of persons and property was the single most important activity of the Nassau County government. This money was used for police services. General government, hospitals, welfare, and highways follow in relative importance expenditure-wise.

This is in marked contrast to 1945 when welfare and general government accounted for 40 per cent of the total amount spent by the county government.

Leaving out the items for capital outlay, police work, health and hospital, and welfare are quite clearly important as major county functions. While health, hospitals, and welfare are essentially entirely county functions, policing is not solely a county government concern. The county Police Department operates as two units, each with individual budgets. "Unit one has county-wide jurisdiction, regardless of town, city or incorporated village lines."[5] Thus headquarters operation is financed in the county budget as an item of county expense supported by and providing services to residents of the entire county. Unit two, known as the Police District "renders police services by the uniformed force through the six precincts to the territory within the Police District, which comprises about 70 per cent of the territory within the county, deriving its maintenance from a tax upon the real property within the district."[6] This explains why the item in the county budget for police is listed as $7,853,157.00 in Table 23 and $4,239,662.24 in Table 24. The territory not within the Police District gets its uniformed police service from local police departments. There are twenty-five such departments in the county. The expense of run-

5 *Annual Report of Nassau County Police Department* (1955), p. 20.
6 *Ibid.*, p. 56.

TABLE 23

Items in County's Budgets, except Sewer Districts	Total
Capital fund—bonds already sold or planned to be sold for necessary permanent improvements. (If the bonds are not sold, the money will not be spent.) Expenditures from this source do not affect the 1956 tax levy	$36,129,017.00
Tax collected by the county to meet state Supreme Court costs	277,545.15
Tax collected in certain villages and unincorporated areas to pay for police service furnished by the county. It is not included in the general tax rate and is not levied in areas having their own police forces	7,853,157.00
County Road Fund—road construction by the county from funds received in motor vehicle registration fees and gasoline taxes	11,189,208.00
Total County Funds outside the county's General Fund Budget	$55,448,927.15

Source: Proposed budget of Nassau County for fiscal year 1956.

TABLE 24

Items in County General Fund	Total
Debt service, a mandatory expense for bonds falling due in 1956 plus interest on the County debt	$ 6,645,975.48
Public welfare and relief, cost of assistance and administration	6,797,145.00
Department of Heath, Meadowbrook Hospital, Nassau County Sanatorium and Division of Laboratories and Research	9,526,925.00
Protection of persons and property	4,239,662.24
Corrections	1,055,768.00
Courts, District Attorney, and Sheriff	2,542,142.86
Permanent improvements	25,000.00
Fixed and other charges, contributions to employees' retirement system, suits and damages, rents, insurance, etc.	2,381,660.50
Education (outside of regular school system)	301,478.45
Reserve for contingencies	400,000.00
Reserve for school districts	1,700,000.00
Board of Supervisors	132,469.00
All other administrative departments	13,650,964.00
Total county general fund	49,399,190.53
Total all County Funds	$104,848,117.67
Sewage Disposal District No. 2—bonds already sold or planned to be sold for construction of the disposal plant, trunk lines and laterals	76,935,000.00
Sewage Disposal District No. 2—for maintenance, operation and debt service charges	2,208,120.90
Sewage Collection Districts—for maintenance, operation and debt service charges	2,412,638.07

Source: Proposed budget of Nassau County for fiscal year 1956.

ning the twenty-five local police departments is provided for in the respective local budgets.

While the government of Nassau County spent more than any other single unit of local government in the county in both 1945 and 1954[7] and was scheduled to be the largest spender in 1956,[8] the total spent by the county officials represented only about 30 per cent of all the money spent in the county by Nassau's 400 units of government both in 1945 and 1954. The 1956 budget figures indicated no significant change in the respective shares of the county and other local units in the total fiscal picture in the county for that year. The town and special district expenditure patterns concern us next.

The county budget for 1956 provided for the expenditures of the amounts shown in Tables 23 and 24.

Town and Special District Expenditures

In 1954 the three towns and the special districts operating therein spent about 10 per cent of the money expended for current and capital purposes in the county and 11 per cent of the total spent for current expenditures. This is approximately the same percentage of the total spent by these units in 1945. That year nearly 10 per cent was used for current and capital outlay and under 10 per cent of the total for current expenditures.

In 1954 town government was spending just over 40 per cent of its funds for highway purposes. Capital outlay and general government took up another 40-odd per cent. Sanitation, recreation, and safety followed in that order. Over a third of the special district money went for sanitation and 28 per cent more for capital outlay. Water and light maintenance represent about another 10 per cent each.

In 1945 highway expenditures also involved 40-odd per cent of the total. General government was nearly 10 per cent more of the total than in 1954 or 31 per cent. Capital outlay was less of the total and recreation and sanitation were about the same as in 1954—about 10 per cent. The special districts were spending

[7] See Tables 16 and 17.

[8] The 1956 budget called for total expenditures of 186 million dollars.

about 5 per cent more of the total money at their disposal for sanitation in 1945 than in 1954. Spending for light maintenance was more than twice as great percentagewise and capital outlay was less than one half of 1 per cent in contrast to 28 per cent of the total spent by the special districts in 1954.

The 1956 town budgets indicate that the pattern of expenditures, whereby the amount of money spent by the town government and the special districts in a particular town are roughly equal, is continuing. The 1956 budget of the town of Hempstead called for the expenditure of $3,527,696.92 for general town services and $2,530,720.98 for maintenance and improvement of highways, or a total to be spent by the town of $6,058,417.90. The tax levy for all special districts in Hempstead was $6,715,495.72 for the year 1956. Highway expenditures still represented the largest single expenditure of the town government. Sanitation was still the largest single item, about one-third of the total amount being spent by the special districts.

The Expenditures of the Villages and Cities

In 1954, the sixty-three villages in Nassau County spent 9.42 per cent of the total monies spent in the county by the county government and all the municipal subdivisions, and 10.71 per cent of the amount of these units expended for current purposes. This is in sharp contrast to 1945 when the respective figures for percentages of total and current expenditures were 16.25 and 16.13.

The sharp drop in the village share of total expenditures of current items by the county and its subdivisions from 16 to 10 per cent is paralleled in the case of the cities. The figures for 1945 gave the latter 7.05 per cent of the total and 6.83 per cent of the amount expended for current items, but in 1954 the figures were 1.76 and 2.04 respectively. Thus we find the towns and special districts now spending a larger share of the money being spent by government in Nassau than the villages do. Moreover, Nassau's two cities spent roughly 40 per cent as much money as all the special districts, more than 260, put together or about one-fifth as much as the total spent by all sixty-three villages together for current items.

A review of the expenditures in Appendix D of each of the units of government located in Nassau shows that four of the sixty-three villages spent more than half of all the money spent by all the villages in 1954. Expenditures by Rockville Centre of about 5.33 million, Freeport just under 4.5 million, Hempstead almost 4 million, Garden City 2.5 million add up to more than $15 million. All the villages in Nassau spent $29 million. Seven villages spent more than two-thirds of the total village expenditures.

The 1954 percentage distribution of expenditures by function for all the villages is shown in Table 25.

The pattern for the cities for the same year is very similar, as the reader can see.

TABLE 25

Percentage Distribution[1] of Expenditures of Villages and Cities by Function in 1954

	Villages	Cities
Capital Outlay	23.72	21.92
Safety	17.97	18.06
General Government	11.63	13.63
Highways	13.83	11.07
Sanitation	12.89	11.84
Recreation	3.24	7.54
Health	.11	.49
Libraries and Museums	1.31	.47
Water Maintenance	4.48	3.71
Light Maintenance	8.56	
Debt Service: Interest	2.28	6.63
All other	.03	4.64

[1] Figures may not add to 100 per cent because of rounding.

Contrasting these data with the situation in 1945 shows that the significant difference is that capital outlay was a relatively minor item of expenditure in 1945 while in 1954 it was more than 20 per cent of the total spent by both the villages and the cities; education is no longer handled by the city fathers; and debt service (interest on which was 13.92 per cent of the city expenditure and 7.41 per cent of village expenditure) had fallen to 6.63 per cent for the city and 2.28 per cent for the villages in 1954.

The village budgets for 1956, like all budgets in Nassau, were higher than in previous years. The budgets in Tables 26 and 27 represent large and small village fiscal plans for 1955–1956.

TABLE 26

Summary Budgets of Village of Garden City for 1953–1955

	1953–54 Budget	1954–55 Budget	1954–55 Expenses	1955–56 Budget
General Government	$ 178,212.00	$ 211,363.00	$ 181,451.70	$ 248,811.00
Highways:				
Maintenance & Care	$ 147,920.00	$ 169,920.00	$ 162,258.95	$ 183,300.00
Street Lighting	72,650.00	74,160.00	72,334.62	85,530.00
Engineering	15,735.00	17,555.00	20,575.74	26,125.00
TOTAL FOR HIGHWAYS	$ 236,305.00	$ 261,635.00	$ 255,169.31	$ 294,955.00
Sanitation & Promotion of Cleanliness:				
Street Cleaning	$ 30,720.00	$ 34,970.00	$ 38,675.29	$ 38,450.00
Sewer System & Disposal Plant	80,860.00	87,420.00	77,338.97	93,570.00
Garbage and Refuse	198,520.00	197,024.00	183,073.12	241,030.00
TOTAL FOR SANITATION & PROMOTION OF CLEANLINESS	$ 310,100.00	$ 319,414.00	$ 299,087.38	$ 373,050.00
Recreation:				
Parks and Playgrounds	$ 105,335.00	$ 113,510.00	$ 108,816.97	$ 127,730.00
Permanent Improvements	$ 17,325.00	$ 31,843.92	$ 26,744.73	$ 30,850.00
Protection of Persons and Property:				
Police Department	$ 303,984.00	$ 358,875.00	$ 326,413.79	$ 392,540.00
Fire Department	134,194.00	134,237.00	129,174.56	144,860.00
Building Department	21,330.00	28,590.00	22,900.52	30,215.00
Civil Defense	5,000.00	5,000.00	1,590.55	5,000.00
TOTAL FOR PROTECTION OF PERSONS AND PROPERTY	$ 464,508.00	$ 526,702.00	$ 480,079.42	$ 572,615.00
Municipal Indebtedness and Interest:				
Retirement of Bonds	$ 65,000.00	$ 90,000.00	$ 90,000.00	$ 90,000.00
LESS: Amount of Reserves (a/c sale of sewer plant land) to be applied toward redemption of Sewer Bonds		13,000.00	13,000.00	11,300.00
	$ 65,000.00	$ 77,000.00	$ 77,000.00	$ 78,700.00
Bond Interest	22,145.00	27,476.25	20,760.85	32,540.67
TOTAL FOR MUNICIPAL INDEBTEDNESS AND INTEREST	$ 87,145.00	$ 104,476.25	$ 97,760.85	$ 111,240.67
TOTAL	**$1,398,930.00**	**$1,568,944.17**	**$1,449,110.36**	**$1,759,251.67**

TABLE 26 (*cont.*)

	1953–54 Budget	1954–55 Budget	1954–55 Expenses	1955–56 Budget
PROVISIONS FOR BALANCING BUDGET:				
Surplus Funds (On Hand or Receivable March 1st)	$ 125,585.74	$ 193,410.14		$ 180,843.56
Transfer from Reserves	12,283.82			
Estimated Revenues	149,637.61	162,755.91		170,400.45
TO BE RAISED BY TAX LEVY	1,111,422.83	1,212,778.12		1,408,007.66
TOTAL	**$1,398,930.00**	**$1,568,944.17**		**$1,759,251.67**
NOTE:				
Assessed Valuation of Taxable Property	$67,769,685	$72,189,174		$78,659,646
Tax Rate per $100 of Assessed Valuation	1.64	1.68		1.79

In the Garden City budget the sum allocated for the protection of persons and property amounts to nearly one-third of the total budget. This is a much higher percentage than is indicated for this function in the figures for all the villages for 1954. This is explained largely by the fact that Garden City is one of the twenty-four of the sixty-three villages in Nassau that have their own police departments and is also one of the few governmental jurisdictions in the county that have paid fire department personnel. Fire protection throughout Nassau is provided for the most part by seventy volunteer fire companies, consisting of over nine thousand men.

The budget of the village of Plandome Manor for 1955–1956 is shown in Table 27.

Unlike Garden City, Plandome Manor does not have its own police; hence the amount for protection of persons and property represents a much smaller share of the budget than for Garden City. On the other hand, highway expenses in Garden City do not nearly approach being 60 per cent of the budget as they are in Plandome Manor. This diversity in kinds and scope of governmental activity is common to Nassau's incorporated areas. A review of the budgets of sixty-five villages and cities for the fiscal years ending in 1956 disclosed budgets ranging in total expenditures from just over $16,000.00 to nearly $2,600,000.00. More than a third of the villages had budgets calling for expenditures of less than $100,000.00 and more than three-fourths of the villages had budgets under $500,000.00.

TABLE 27

Budget of Village of Plandome Manor for 1955–1956

Revenues		
Property taxes, ass. val. $3,645,609 @ $.12 per $100	$ 4374.73	
Port Washington Fire Dist. tax, insurance, ass. val. $915,160 @ $.16 per $100	1464.25	
State Aid	2675.30	
Mortgage Taxes	1000.00	
Surplus as of February 28, 1955	9105.18	
		$18,619.46
Disbursements		
GENERAL GOVERNMENT		
Board of Trustees		
Auditing	$ 125.00	
Office & Other	1675.00	
Board of Appeals	125.00	
Zoning Expenses	50.00	
Legal Expenses	250.00	
Engineering Expenses	500.00	
Village Clerk		
Compensation	1020.00	
Office & Other	300.00	
Election: adv. & printing	100.00	
Contingent Fund	500.00	
Miscellaneous	100.15	
		$ 4,745.15
HIGHWAY		
Street Commissioner	$ 500.00	
Wages—roadwork	3646.35	
Street Cleaning	1400.00	
Truck hire	1550.00	
Materials and supplies	2200.00	
Snow and ice removal	1250.00	
Insurance	700.00	
Street lighting	625.00	
Building Inspector's Fees		
		$11,871.35
CONSERVATION OF HEALTH		40.00
PROTECTION, PERSONS & PROPERTY		
Port Washington Fire Dept. & Insurance		1,462.96
CIVIL DEFENSE		500.00
		$18,619.46

School District Expenditures

The residents of Nassau County spend more money for education than for any other single governmental activity. In 1954, Nassau's sixty-two different school boards spent varying amounts of money for their respective schools, the sum total for all being $111,659,763.52 or 48.97 per cent of all the money spent for current and capital expenditures by the county government and all the municipal subdivisions in the county and 46.40 per cent of all the money spent for current items. Comparable figures for 1945 for these respective purposes were, for the former, 34.34 per cent, and the latter, 35.02 per cent.

In terms of total amounts of money spent by governmental units in the county, the local school boards spend nearly half of all the money spent in Nassau County for local governmental purposes. These boards are unsalaried, part time, and highly dependent upon the professional staff of their respective schools in matters of educational policy and fiscal planning. The expenditure pattern in 1954 differs from that of 1945 in that the amount spent for capital improvements in the later period is more than one-third of the total spent by the school boards. In 1945, this figure was less than 3 per cent.

TABLE 28

Percentage Distribution of School District Expenditures in 1945 and 1954

	1954 School Districts	1945 School Districts
Education	59.99	97.95
Capital Outlay	36.48	2.05
Debt Service	3.53	

As might be expected, there is a great variation in the amount of money spent by each of the sixty-odd school districts. The average expenditures of school districts in the county are far in excess of the average expenditures of the incorporated places in Nassau. For example, more than half, thirty-nine, of the school districts spent over one million dollars each for operating expenses alone in the fiscal year, 1954–1955. The 1955–1956 budgets indicated that only ten of the villages and cities planned expenditures about or above one million dollars for the fiscal years ending in 1956.

Since education consumes such a large part of expenditures in Nassau, perhaps it might be meaningful to explore this item a bit further. Data filed with the state comptroller's office show that $123,059,900.29 was spent by Nassau school boards for current, capital outlay, and debt service expenditures in 1953–1954 as opposed to a comparable figure of $16,225,552.71 for 1944–1945.

Figures obtained by the author from the state Department of Education indicate that in 1954–1955 just under 161 million dollars was spent for the purpose of educating Nassau's youth. This is an increase of nearly one-third over the preceding year. This figure of $160,870,072.63 is made up of $83,290,648.96 for current expenses, $13,504,507.73 for debt service, $2,551,883.00 and $61,-523,032.94 for capital outlay. In other words, roughly 40 per cent of the money spent for education in 1955 went for capital outlay.

The marked increase in the cost of education is also reflected in the following comparison of the cost per pupil based on the current expense less special schools divided by the total average daily attendance.

In the school fiscal year 1945–1946, the amount spent per capita ranged from $162.26 at one end of the scale to $1,030.99 at the other.

Amount Spent per Pupil	Number of Districts Spending This Amount
162 to 200	17
201 to 300	29
301 to 400	13
401 to 500	3
501 to 600	3
Above 600	1

The average expenditure was $279.59. In this year roughly two-thirds of the districts (43 out of 66) spent less than the average.

In 1950–1951, the range per capita was $150.24 to $887.98:

Amount Spent per Pupil	Number of Districts Spending This Amount
150.24 to 200	3
201 to 300	21
301 to 400	19
401 to 500	12
501 to 600	5
601 to 700	3
Above 700	1

The average expenditure was $359.46. In 1950–1951, 38 of the 64 districts or 60 per cent spent less than the average.

In 1954–1955, the range per capita was $298.13 to $1,062.41.

Amount Spent per Pupil	Number of Districts Spending This Amount
298 to 300	1
301 to 400	18
401 to 500	16
501 to 600	15
601 to 700	4
701 to 800	5
Above 800	2

The average expenditure was $491.60. More than 50 per cent or 32 of 61 of the school districts spent less than the average. The great variation in the expenditures per pupil in Nassau's schools is further evidenced in Table 15 on page 53.

Most home owners are fully aware of the fact that school costs have been going up.[9] They are quite conscious of the new school buildings springing up throughout the county. They are perhaps not as much aware of the fact that school taxes are still a long way from being static and that a great deal more building is still to be done by many of Nassau's school systems. A slight insight into the future of school expenditures can be gathered by consideration of the budget figures of School District 18 for 1953–1954, 1954–1955, 1955–1956 and 1956–1957. These are the budget totals of a school district whose increase in expenditures and tax rates has been one of the more modest in the county.

[9] See Section B, The Revenue Pattern, below.

The 1953–1954 budget called for expenditures of $1,600,683.25 and the budget for 1956–1957, three years later, resulted in an expenditure of roughly $2,700,000.00, an increase of about $1,100,-000.00. By 1958–1959 the school budget in Garden City had increased almost 100 per cent over 1953–1954.

In 1955–1956 it had increased roughly 100 per cent over 1950–1951. In that year the budget was $1,157,673.25, and the 1955–1956 budget involved the expenditure of $2,305,340.00. It is interesting that there is no real difference in the budgets as proposed and the budgets as adopted.

The budget for 1945–1946 for District 18 provided $661,748.25 for the school operations. The budget for 1956–1957 was $2,688,-242.00 or more than 2 million dollars more—an increase of more than 300 per cent. This increase, strikingly, is less than half the rate of increase of total expenditures for education in Nassau from 1944–1945 to 1953–1954. The rate of increase here was 657 per cent.

Fire Districts

In 1945, about one quarter of the funds spent by the fire districts was for capital outlay. The expenditures in 1954 for this purpose were approximately the same percentage of the total. While the fire districts are spending nearly 9 per cent, $1,330,-144.27, of all the money spent in Nassau County for the protection of persons and property, they are spending a smaller part of the total amount spent by all the units in Nassau than they did in 1945.

B. THE REVENUE PATTERN

The revenues of the units of local government in Nassau County are derived primarily from the tax on real property and fiscal aid from state government. In 1954 slightly more than one-half of the revenue collected in Nassau came from the property tax and just a little under one-half from several other sources including state aid. The total of $181,593,247.58 identified in Table 29[10]

[10] See Appendix G for 1945 figures.

includes 54 per cent from the real estate tax, 18 per cent from state aid, 10 per cent from assessments, 2 per cent from federal aid, 1 per cent from local non-property taxes and 13 per cent from other sources such as fines, fees, licenses, etc. In other words 74 per cent of Nassau revenues can be traced to the property tax and fiscal aid from higher governmental jurisdictions.

In comparing the two charts (Table 29 and Appendix G), one is struck by the degree to which the relative dependence on the various sources of revenue seems to have shifted in the last ten years.

The impression that the dependence upon the property tax has declined to such a marked degree as seems to be the case is in a way false. The income from taxes on real property actually consists of the taxes on property for general county or village purposes as well as those special assessments levied in the towns to provide particular districts with sanitation or lighting services. As the reader can see below, nearly 40 per cent of the revenue of the towns comes from assessments. When the dependence of the community upon the real property tax and assessment together is considered for 1945 and 1954, the shift in the relative dependence upon taxes on property as a source of revenue is not quite as pronounced as it might at first glance appear.

A comparison of the 1954 pattern with that of 1945 shows that in 1954 the property tax and assessments represented two-thirds of the sources of all revenue, a drop since 1945. State and federal aid and local non-property taxes and income from other sources have increased. Note, however, that shifts in dependence upon particular sources of revenue since 1945 have been varied depending upon the unit of government involved.

Another development of considerable interest that characterized the period from 1945 to 1954 was the great increase in the share that income from governmental borrowing constituted of the total monies being raised by Nassau's governmental jurisdictions. In 1954 the total revenue of all the units of government in the county represented just under two-thirds of the total income from revenue and borrowing combined. In 1945 revenue represented 96 per cent of this total. The percentage distribution of income by sources for 1954 is shown in Appendix F. The large percentage of

TABLE 29

Income [1] by Source for Nassau County and All Units Located Therein for Fiscal Years Ending in 1954

Source	Total	County	Cities	Towns	Villages	School Districts	Fire Districts
Borrowing and Revenue	$278,483,787.19	$71,862,671.24	$4,470,380.16	$26,367,172.50	$28,471,006.06	$144,688,212.02	$2,624,345.21
Borrowings	96,890,539.61	19,012,031.01	547,000.00	7,750,977.79	8,947,080.24	60,539,586.21	93,864.36
Revenue	181,593,247.58	52,850,640.23	3,923,380.16	18,616,194.71	19,523,925.82	84,148,625.81	2,530,480.85
Assessments	$ 19,163,797.02	$ 9,067,927.17	$	$ 7,373,205.49	$ 769,972.46	$	$1,952,691.90
Local Non-Property Taxes	2,859,760.79	2,657,360.85	139,981.30			62,418.64	
State Aid	33,495,685.40	5,817,987.43	284,213.50	3,726,005.72	1,720,662.89	21,946,815.86	
Real Estate Tax	98,220,453.81	28,174,303.64	2,216,866.68	3,827,546.90	11,246,805.27	52,754,931.32	
Federal Aid	4,086,087.56	1,684,793.94	863.60	432.76		2,399,997.26	
Other	23,767,463.00	5,448,267.20	1,281,455.08	3,689,003.84	5,786,435.20	6,984,462.73	577,788.95

[1] Does not include transfers, trust and investment transactions, or the balance at the beginning of the year.

Source: Figures derived from New York State Comptroller, **Special Report on Municipal Affairs,** Legislative Document (1955) No. 33A (Albany: Fort Orange Press, 1955).

the money derived from borrowings being spent by the school districts is worth noting.

The revenue pattern of each of the classes of government for 1945 and 1954 was as follows:

TABLE 30

Percentage Distribution[1] of Revenue by Source for Nassau County in 1945 and 1954

	1945	1954
Real Estate Tax	77.21	53.31
State and Federal Aid	8.46	14.19
Shared tax	4.37	
Other	9.95	10.31
Assessments		17.16
Non-property tax		5.03

[1] Figures may not add to 100 per cent because of rounding.

While the dependency upon the property tax has decreased, the role of assessments in the total picture is considerably greater than it was in 1945. The general fund summary contained in the 1956 county budget (see Table 31), calls for more than 60 per cent of the revenue to be met from the tax levy. This would seem to indicate a possible reversal of the trend toward less dependency on the property tax.

TABLE 31

General Fund Summary—County Government Revenues

	Actual 1954	Budget 1955	Forecast 1956
Available Cash Balances	$ 6,386,449.70	$ 6,408,100.00	$ 5,284,900.00
Collection of Tax Arrears	2,377,488.25	1,085,000.00	1,190,000.00
Tax Interest and Penalties	511,293.89	151,000.00	155,000.00
Departmental and Miscellaneous Receipts	4,390,518.85	4,448,036.00	4,643,033.00
Federal and State Aid	5,044,161.82	5,391,771.00	5,835,841.74
Collection of Current Year's Tax Levy	26,115,729.95	27,021,524.31	32,229,123.79
Pari-Mutual Tax—Belmont Park	2,070,377.24	975,000.00	
Admission Tax—Belmont Park	284,927.96	275,000.00	285,000.00
Admission Tax—Roosevelt Raceway	302,055.65	300,000.00	325,000.00
Sewage Disposal—District No. 2	68,020.87	170,000.00	55,000.00
Total Receipts	$47,551,024.18	$46,225,431.31	$50,002,898.53

Source: Proposed budget of Nassau County for year ending December 1956.

TABLE 32

Percentage Distribution [1] of Revenue by Source for Nassau's Two Cities in 1945 and 1954

	1945	1954
Real Estate Tax [1]	61.49	56.50
State and Federal Aid	6.14	7.27
Local Non-Property Tax	.46	3.56
Other	22.64	32.67
Shared Tax	3.02	
Assessments	6.25	

[1] The fact that Nassau's two cities no longer support the city school programs out of their city budget funds may account for the shift in the relative amount of the contribution of the real estate tax to the total revenue.

TABLE 33

Percentage Distribution [1] of Revenue by Source for Nassau's Three Towns in 1945 and 1954

	1945	1954
Real Estate Tax	19.54	20.56
Assessments	40.93	39.60
Other	18.59	19.82
State and Federal Aid	1.35	20.02
Shared Tax	19.59	

[1] Figures may not add to 100 per cent because of rounding.

Interestingly enough the towns in Nassau show a smaller change between 1945 and 1954 in terms of relative dependence on particular sources of revenue than do the county and cities. The percentage of the total aid received from the state has declined. The role of the districts is reflected in the amounts derived from assessments.

TABLE 34

Percentage Distribution [1] of Revenue by Source for Nassau's Sixty-three Villages in 1945 and 1954

	1945	1954
Real Estate Tax	62.84	57.59
State Aid	.26	8.81
Assessments	1.29	3.95
Other	24.81	29.64
Shared Tax	10.70	

[1] Figures may not add to 100 per cent because of rounding.

The villages, like the towns, are receiving less fiscal aid relatively speaking than they did in 1945. Other sources of revenue have taken up the slack growing out of the decreased dependency on the property tax. It is necessary to point out, however, that the figures above represent the dependency upon particular sources of revenue in terms of the total amount of revenue received from each source by all sixty-three villages put together. The revenue patterns of many, if not all, of the villages as individual units are not to be assumed to follow this pattern of the total identified above.

Here is testimony of the varied nature of village revenue patterns with respect to dependency upon the property tax. The Garden City budget for 1955–1956 called for 80 per cent of the revenue to be raised from the property tax, while in the village of Freeport budget the percentage of the total to be derived from the real estate tax was less than two-thirds of the total.

TABLE 35

Revenue to Balance Garden City Budgets

	1953–54	%	1954–55	%	1955–56	%
Current Surplus	$ 125,585.74	9.0	$ 193,410.14	12.3	$ 180,843.56	10.3
Transfer from Reserves	12,283.82	0.9				
Estimated Revenue	149,637.61	10.7	162,755.91	10.4	170,400.45	9.7
Tax Levy	1,111,422.83	79.4	1,212,778.12	77.3	1,408,007.66	80.0
	$1,398,930.00	100.0	$1,568,944.17	100.0	$1,759,251.67	100.0

Source: Analyses of the tentative 1955–1956 budget of the incorporated village of Garden City, April 6, 1955.

TABLE 36

Summary of Budget of the Incorporated Village of Freeport for Year 1955–1956

	Total	General Fund
Appropriations	$1,620,125.76	$1,620,125.76
Less:		
Estimated Revenues, other than Real Estate	421,131.38	421,131.38
Appropriated Cash Surplus	152,579.38	152,579.38
	573,710.76	573,710.76
Balance of Appropriations to be Raised by Real Estate Tax Levy	$1,046,415.00	$1,046,415.00
Assessed Valuation, $59,795,143.00; Tax Rate, 1.75.		

Source: Budget for village of Freeport for 1955–1956.

The School Districts

The school districts still depend very heavily upon the property tax for revenue. The degree to which individual districts depend upon this source, as with the villages, varies from district to district. This variation is also true of fiscal assistance from higher levels of government.

The Fire Districts

The fire districts seem to be less dependent upon the property tax, with additional revenue coming from other sources.

The Distribution of Receipts of Units of Government

School districts in Nassau spend more than any other single unit of government there and likewise receive a larger share of the income than the county, the cities, the towns, the villages, or the fire districts do.

In 1954 the total amount of money, $278,483,787.19, received as borrowings and revenue by Nassau County and its municipal subdivisions, was distributed in the following manner:

TABLE 37

Percentage Distribution [1] of Kinds of Income by Units of Government in 1954

	Borrow-ing and Revenue	Revenue	Borrow-ing	Assess-ments	Local Non-Prop. Tax	State Aid	Real Estate Tax	Fed. Aid	Other
Total	100.00	100.00	100.00	100.00	100.00	100.00	100.00	100.00	100.00
County	25.80	29.10	19.62	47.31	92.92	17.37	28.68	41.23	22.92
Cities	1.61	2.16	.57		4.89	.85	2.25	.02	5.39
Towns	9.46	10.25	8.00	38.48		11.12	3.90	.01	15.52
Villages	10.23	10.75	9.23	4.02		5.13	11.45		24.34
School Districts	51.95	46.34	62.48		2.19	65.52	53.71	58.74	29.38
Fire Districts	.94	1.39	.10	10.19					2.44

[1] Figures may not add to 100 per cent because of rounding.

The school districts received 52 per cent of the total receipts; 46 per cent of the total revenue; 62 per cent of the money from borrowings; 65 per cent of the state aid, 58 per cent of the federal aid, 54 per cent of the real estate tax, and only 2 per cent of the local non-property tax.

Note that each unit of government receives revenue from the real estate tax. The relatively less significant role of the county, the city, and the villages in contrast to the increasingly large part being played by the special districts and the school districts in the total scheme of things in Nassau, so clearly apparent in the discussion of expenditures, is just as obvious in the revenue picture.

In the following table the decreasing share of the county, cities, and villages in the total revenue is readily apparent.

TABLE 38

Percentage Distribution [1] of Total Revenue by Units of Government

	1945	1954
County	33.58	29.10
Cities	7.16	2.16
Villages	16.14	10.75
Fire Districts	.98	1.39
School Districts	33.07	46.34
Towns	9.06	10.25

[1] Figures may not add to 100 per cent because of rounding.

The increasing share of the towns, special districts, and school districts is also quite clear.

This pattern is repeated, with some variation, in terms of revenues derived from the real estate tax.

TABLE 39

Percentage Distribution [1] of Revenues from Real Estate Tax

	1945	1954
County	38.59	28.68
Cities	6.55	2.25
Villages	15.10	11.45
Fire Districts	1.35	
School Districts	35.78	53.71
Towns	2.63	3.90

[1] Figures may not add to 100 per cent because of rounding.

The percentages of the real estate tax listed above do not include revenues from assessments.

Current Surplus as Income

It is difficult to move on to the next question of tax rates without mentioning a unique characteristic of budgets of the units of government serving Nassau County. The writer found budget after budget for the fiscal period ending in 1956 with rather large appropriated cash surplus items listed as significant items of income by which budgets were to be balanced. The county government started 1956 with an estimated cash balance amounting to 10 per cent of the total of the general fund.[11] Garden City [12] started 1953–1954 with a surplus of 9 per cent, 1954–1955 with a surplus of 12.3 per cent, and 1955–1956 with a surplus of 10.3 per cent. The town of Hempstead had an estimated unexpended balance as of December 31, 1955 of about 30 per cent of the total of the estimated revenue in the budget for general town services for 1956.[13] Nor was this a unique case. The 1954 budget for the same town had an estimated unexpended balance on December 31, 1953, of $1,061,442.17. The total estimated revenue and balance for that budget was $3,161,270.17.[14] One village budget called for disbursements of $30,165.00 to be balanced by state aid of $2,365.09, a property tax levy of $8,060.74, and cash on hand amounting to $19,739.17.

Tax Rates

The resident of Nassau County is subject to a tax levy on his property by the several governmental jurisdictions providing him with services. The number of governmental units imposing a tax on the home owner or property owner of course varies with loca-

[11] See Table 31 (page 85).

[12] See Table 35 (page 87).

[13] The budget called for the expenditure of $3,527,696.92 for general town services. This figure does not include $2,530,720.98 for maintenance and improvement of highways.

[14] See Appendix J.

tion of the property. Residents of villages or cities are subject to a different number of taxes than residents of unincorporated areas. As was indicated earlier in this study, the entire tax burden on the property owner of Nassau must always be considered in terms of the sum total of real estate taxes levied by many jurisdictions on his holdings. The tax rates on real property in Nassau have been increasing steadily since 1945, with the school tax rate leading the field. The resident of the established villages has seen the least pronounced increase in his total tax rate, yet even in this situation the rise has been pronounced (see Appendix I).

In 1945, 50 of the 63 villages had a tax rate of under $1.00 per 100 dollars of assessment, 25 had a tax rate under 50 cents and only 3 had a tax rate over $1.50. In 1956, 5 had a tax over $2.00. Nine were between $1.50 and $2.00 and 35 had a tax rate of $1.00 or more.

The school tax rates have taken the most pronounced jumps over the 1945 figures. The following tax rates show the districts in the town of Hempstead paying over $4.00 per $100 in 1955–1956.

TABLE 40

Comparison of School Tax Rates for $100 Valuation for School Years 1944–1945 and 1955–1956

School District	1944–45 Tax Rate	1955–56 Tax Rate
No. 5 Jerusalem	.25	4.65
7 Bellmore	1.34	4.14
13 Malverne	1.16	4.55
14 Woodmere-Hewlett	1.203	4.32
17 Franklin Square	1.38	4.19
23 Wantagh	1.24	4.40
24 Valley Stream	1.17	4.70
25 Merrick	1.18	4.16
26 Island Trees	.50	4.42
27 West Hempstead	1.11	4.26
29 North Merrick	1.53	4.38
30 Valley Stream	1.26	4.61

Twelve of the 32 districts in the town of Hempstead were paying more than $40 per $1000 assessment. The districts in the same town paying less than $30 per $1000 and their tax rates were:

TABLE 41

Comparison of School Tax Rates for $100 Valuation for School Years 1944–1945 and 1955–1956

School District	1944–1945 Tax Rate	1955–1956 Tax Rate
No. 1 Hempstead	.93	2.28
18 Garden City	1.06	2.78
28 Long Beach	1.35	2.826
31 Island Park	1.29	2.875
9 Freeport	1.26	2.92
19 East Rockaway	1.41	2.99

These six school districts are all located in the well-established older communities. This is in contrast to the majority of the twelve listed in Table 40, which are situated in areas of great postwar expansion.

There is every reason to believe that these rates of over $4 per hundred will in the not too distant future be $5 and $6. Note the change in rates from the year 1954–1955 to 1955–1956 in the same town.

TABLE 42

Town of Hempstead—Changes in School Tax Rates between 1954–1955 and 1955–1956

SD	Location	1954–1955 Tax Rate	1955–1956 Tax Rate	Increase or Decrease
1	Hempstead	$2.10	$2.28	+ .18
2	Uniondale	2.86	3.19	+ .33
3	East Meadow	2.92	3.423	+ .503
4	North Bellmore	3.85	3.85	
5	Jerusalem	3.67	4.65	+ .98
6	Seaford	3.52	3.714	+ .194
7	Bellmore	4.31	4.14	− .17
8	Roosevelt	2.76	3.42	+ .66
9	Freeport	2.87	2.92	+ .05
10	Baldwin	3.24	3.34	+ .10
11	Oceanside	3.50	3.94	+ .44
12	North Lynbrook	2.73	3.15	+ .42
13	Malverne	3.67	4.55	+ .88
14	Woodmere-Hewlett	3.767	4.32	+ .553
15	Lawrence	2.984	3.23	+ .246
16	Elmont	3.30	3.80	+ .50
17	Franklin Square	3.61	4.19	+ .58
18	Garden City	2.32	2.78	+ .46

TABLE 42 (*cont.*)

Town of Hempstead—Changes in School Tax Rates between 1954–1955 and 1955–1956

SD	Location	1954–1955 Tax Rate	1955–1956 Tax Rate	Increase or Decrease
19	East Rockaway	2.93	2.99	+ .06
20	Lynbrook	3.30	3.13	− .17
21	Rockville Centre	2.98	3.42	+ .44
22	Floral Park (Jt.)	2.82	3.04	+ .22
23	Wantagh	4.45	4.40	− .05
24	Valley Stream	3.65	4.70	+1.05
25	Merrick	4.27	4.16	− .11
26	Island Trees	3.46	4.42	+ .96
27	West Hempstead	3.53	4.26	+ .73
28	Long Beach	2.629	2.806	+ .177
29	North Merrick	4.17	4.38	+ .21
30	Valley Stream	3.40	4.61	+1.21
31	Island Park	2.42	2.875	+ .435
NH1	Westbury (Jt.)	2.71	2.73	+ .02
NH5	New Hyde Park (Jt.)	2.953	3.654	+ .701

Other tax rates of such units as the special districts have also gone up, although not as rapidly and dramatically. The wide differences in tax rates to be found in the villages and school districts are just as evident in terms of the multitude of special districts.

Part III
Summary

The governmental structure of Nassau County is confronted with the following considerations:

1. Nassau has emerged as a county-wide community whose problems and their solutions transcend the existing political boundaries, and whose problems are somewhat similar to those of the larger metropolitan area.

2. There is a need for thorough reorganization of the existing pattern of government, not only to reduce the fragmentation of governmental authority, but also to provide the latest in modern management techniques for Nassau public officials.

3. Any change in the existing fabric of government must await a comprehensive review of the entire matter by a county charter revision commission.

The Regional Problems Are Mirrored at the County Level

Recent years have witnessed a growing realization that the solution to metropolitan problems requires a regional approach. Should it not also be abundantly clear that the solution to county-wide problems requires a regional approach? The interdependence of the parts of the metropolitan area of New York is mirrored in the community of Nassau. The writer is struck by the degree to which the following quotations dealing with the fiscal problems of the metropolitan area parallel his findings on Nassau. Substitution of the word "county" for the words in italics is all that is needed to say this is the nature of the fiscal problem in Nassau.

> The financing of local government in *these focal centers of the State's* economy is more comprehensive than raising revenue, incurring and re-

paying debt and making expenditures. It is an integral part of the making and carrying out of plans and programs for performing functions and services and providing the necessary facilities; it involves determinations of fiscal policy respecting priorities in the spending of available income; organization of fiscal administration; fiscal management decisions on the most economical and efficient way of accomplishing objectives. It is influenced by the way in which a *metropolitan* area develops and changes, by the location of industrial and residential areas, and by the resultant need for such basic services and facilities as arterial highways, parking and terminal facilities, mass transportation, water supply, sanitation, schools, and the like. And it is affected enormously by whether such development is haphazard or in keeping with a comprehensive plan.

The potential fiscal capacity in all or most of the *State's urban areas* appears to be sufficient to meet these local government financial requirements. The cost of *urban* government is high, but there are the offsetting factors of concentration of industrial and business enterprise and a relatively high level of personal income. The means to use these resources well for the common needs of the area, however, are in need of further development.[1]

This state report continues:

There is no local public agency with area-wide responsibility for planning and coordinating development and for providing basic services that are needed by the areas as a whole.[2] . . .

The taxable resources of a given area are not distributed among the political subdivisions providing government in the area in proportion to their respective needs.[3] . . .

Underlying this lack of comprehensiveness, and explaining much about the nature of the problem, is the fact that the counties, cities and towns are long established institutions, that local home rule is greatly cherished, and that the State Government, in its special objective over the past several years of strengthening local government, in the main has followed cooperative rather than coercive policies.[4]

The appropriateness of these statements to Nassau is striking.

1 New York State Temporary Commission on the Fiscal Affairs of State Government, *A Program for Continued Progress in Fiscal Management,* Vol. 1 (Albany, 1955), p. 141.

2 *Ibid.,* p. 141.

3 *Ibid.,* p. 141.

4 *Ibid.,* p. 142.

The Need for Governmental Reorganization in Nassau

The governmental structure of Nassau County and its subdivisions is inadequate to meet the demands of its present, let alone its future, population. The present pattern of government has existed with slight change since 1938. At that time it represented a recognized compromise between a form of government to meet the needs of the increasingly less rural county and the traditional governmental apparatus of rural America. In short, the partially adequate governmental structure of 1938 is as efficient in meeting the governmental needs of today as the propeller-driven aircraft of the thirties would be in handling the transportation demands of this atomic age.

> If the social and economic context had not changed so quickly or so drastically, the deliberate responses of governmental structure and procedure to new conditions might have been adequate. But change has come through rapid surges rather than through a gradual advance, and many of the difficulties of the present day derive from the inability of a government designed for different and simpler problems to meet the present demands on it.[5]

What are the present day demands on Nassau's semi-rural governmental structure? The demands are those of a dynamic, rapidly urbanizing community with a population of over one million people. This area of 274 square miles is the fastest growing suburban county in America. Its problems are not in any sense reduced by its being part of the most heavily populated metropolitan area in the United States and bordering on one of the world's great cities, New York.

The resident of Nassau County is provided with the necessary services of local government by a combination of several of the approximately four hundred units of government now functioning in the county. As one expert on government puts it in considering this excessive fragmentation of the governmental process, "Duplication, confusion and divided leadership exact a high toll.

[5] Temporary State Commission to Study the Organizational Structure of the Government of the City of New York, *Four Steps to Better Government*, Part II (Albany, 1953), p. 29.

But above all, the system of splintered government creates an invisible form of government, making it extremely difficult for the average citizen to keep informed as to just how he is being governed."[6]

With respect to money being spent for governmental services, the Nassau County government, the 3 towns, the 2 cities, the 63 villages, the 62 school districts, and the more than 260 special districts serving the county residents, are engaged in an expensive governmental operation. The total amount spent by all these units in 1954 exceeded one-quarter of a billion dollars and in 1958 probably exceeded 400 million dollars. As indicated in the body of this report, the figures for 1954 represent an increase of more than 400 per cent over comparable expenditure figures for 1945. It is apparent that the cost of governing Nassau is climbing at a rate in excess of that of the extraordinary population growth and is destined to continue to do so. This is not to imply that government is necessarily less efficient today than in 1945 but recognition of the fact that the combination of inflation, greater demand for services in an urban community, and population growth account for pronounced changes in the expenditure pattern.

The fragmentation of governmental responsibility is sharply dramatized in the review of governmental expenditures treated in Part II. In 1954 the county government spent about 30 per cent of the total amount of money spent by county government and its municipal subdivisions. In other words, the only government with county-wide jurisdiction is spending approximately one-third of the money being expended for local governmental purposes in the county. Moreover, this total sum of more than a quarter of a billion dollars is so allocated for the various governmental functions being performed that sole county responsibility for particular functions is restricted sharply to a narrow range including health, hospitals, and welfare, which are not the main items in the county expenditure pattern. Education, costing nearly half the amount spent for current governmental purposes, is provided for by the 62 local districts. Police and fire protection are provided by county, city, village, town, and special district personnel.

[6] Wallace S. Sayre, unpublished speech before Garden City Democratic Club, March 22, 1956.

The county spends roughly 60 per cent of the money being spent for public safety in the county. This characteristic of divided responsibility for particular governmental services in the county is also common to highway, sanitation, water, recreation, and other governmental activities.

Some perhaps feel the way the Municipal Consultant Service did in 1934 when it reported to the County Board of Supervisors that

> We believe that the solution of the problem of the areas of government in Nassau County is to be found in the proper adjustment of their functions. Recognizing the necessity for the continued existence of county, towns and villages, we would give to the county those duties which it can best perform, leaving to the towns and villages those which they can best perform. This seems to us the sensible and constructive policy, and we consider it defensible against those who would completely revolutionize the structure of county government as well as against those who are prepared to resist any change.[7]

This report also touched another aspect of the problem of trying to govern an urban area with a semi-rural form of government. In considering the point treated earlier in this paper, the problem of the property owner being confronted with the total weight of the taxes levied upon his property by all the layers of government serving him, this 1934 survey presented a chart showing one village under its load of governmental expense. Its comment was: "We have here an impressive monument to man's lack of wit in arranging for the satisfaction of his communal needs. It is heavy on whoever lies beneath it."[8]

The serious overlapping and duplication of services evident in 1934 is considerably more serious and duplicative today. The increase in governmental units by nearly one hundred, 301 to 399, between 1933 and 1956 speaks for itself. The dependence upon the property tax and total property tax rates representing the aggregate of county, town, and district rates, of up to 8 and more per $100 assessment sharply confirms the necessity to heed the admonition advanced in 1934. "It is time, before graver losses

[7] Municipal Consultant Service of the National Municipal League, *The Government of Nassau County* (Mineola, 1934), p. 5.
[8] *Ibid.*, p. 15.

are suffered and before tax burdens become prohibitive, to take the necessary measures to give the people of Nassau County a well organized, efficient and economical governmental system."[9]

While the initial purpose of this study was to review the expenditure and revenue patterns of the county and its municipal subdivisions, the writer soon found himself involved in budgets, executive powers, legislative actions, and provisions or lack of provisions for managerial assistance to both the executive and legislative branches of government. Where the study of fiscal affairs is involved, one soon finds himself in a position of seeing much more than dollars spent and revenue received. The writer contends that Nassau's governmental system (the approximately 400 units) can be further characterized as a semi-rural and inadequate system by its adherence to the long ballot, the supremacy of the legislature, the relatively weak chief executive, and the inadequate staffing of the executive with all of the most modern managerial tools.

The residents of Nassau elect many people to the various local offices, from the county level down to the district level. While the position of the county executive in comparison with the executive at other levels in the county is a strong one, it can hardly be compared with the executive power and responsibility of the mayor of New York City, for example. "The position of the county executive is not an executive office in the usual sense. Its occupant does not stand out as the visible leader of the executive branch, taking responsibility for programs and policies, and being held accountable for the mistakes of himself and his subordinates." [10] Nor does it appear that the county executive, or any other executive in the county for that matter, is adequately equipped with all the latest tools of modern governmental management.

These points are made primarily to stress the need for a solution to the county's problems that is broader and more inclusive than simply one of reallocating functions. They also suggest the inabilities of fragmented government to benefit to the fullest extent from the tools of modern management, i.e., performance budgeting, management analysis, etc. The writer did not find

9 *Ibid.*
10 Sayre, *op. cit.*

even one person in the county government system with the title of budget director. Nor did a review of the many budgets involved indicate any widespread acceptance of the concept of performance budgeting. Evidently there is no comprehensive program in the county whereby the county government and the lower units of government can benefit from either periodic or constant review of the management techniques being employed to achieve more efficient governmental service.

RECOMMENDATIONS

It is apparent that the existing governmental system based on the division of governmental authority and responsibility amongst four hundred units of government represents an excessive fragmentation of the governmental process. The cost of this in duplication, confusion, and the inability to identify responsibility is also obvious. The solution to the problem is not so easy to arrive at.

In light of the fact that the answer to Nassau's fragmental government involves many basic constitutional questions relative to the question of home rule, etc. it is imperative that a most thorough and comprehensive study be made of the adequacy of the system of government currently in operation in Nassau. This should be done in time to permit consideration of whatever constitutional changes the researchers might deem necessary before the next session of the state legislature.

To this end this report recommends that a charter revision commission be appointed with adequate financial resources to employ expert help, to study the entire question of the government of Nassau County and its municipal subdivisions—especially of their adequacy to meet the present and future needs of the residents of the county. This commission should be instructed to prepare a report of its findings and proposed changes and to draft legislation to implement them, for submission to the appropriate authorities.

The writer hopes that this study of the governments of Nassau County and the local units therein, and their expenditure and revenue patterns in 1945 and 1954, has served to point up some of the issues with which a charter revision commission must deal. These include such questions as:

1. Should all governmental services in Nassau be provided by the county government? If so, what constitutional changes are necessary?

2. Should the county retain the existing layers of governmental authority but reallocate the functions of government?

Should police, fire, water, sanitation, and education fall more under county jurisdiction than they now do?

3. Is the price of home rule too high? Does the citizen understand the price being paid? Is the citizen willing to pay that price?

4. Can the needs for comprehensive planning and allocation of existing and potential resources according to priority needs be met under the existing fragmentation of the governmental process?

5. Where is the increased revenue to meet the increasing expenditures to come from? Is it from more state aid, the real estate tax, or additional and new sources?

6. What economies in government could be secured by improved general executive management at all levels?

7. Is the uniqueness of Nassau County such that its governmental system should be at variance with that of other counties in the state?

Appendix A

Population of Nassau County and All Units of Government Located Therein in 1940, 1950, and 1954

Unit of Government	1940	1950	1954
Nassau County	406,748	672,765	966,841
Town of Hempstead	259,318	448,092	618,065
Town of North Hempstead	83,385	142,613	184,060
Town of Oyster Bay	42,594	82,060	164,716
City of Glen Cove	12,415	15,130	19,296
City of Long Beach	9,036	15,586	17,999
Villages of			
Baxter Estates	760	862	934
Bayville	1,516	1,981	2,599
Bellerose	1,317	1,134	1,146
Brookville	204	337	439
Cedarhurst	5,463	6,051	6,544
Centre Island	134	199	253
Cove Neck	130	200	212
East Hills	343	2,547	4,542
East Rockaway	5,610	7,970	8,933
East Williston	1,152	1,734	2,375
Farmingdale	3,524	4,492	5,771
Floral Park	12,950	14,582	17,596
Flower Hill	666	1,948	3,056
Freeport	20,410	24,680	28,359
Garden City	11,223	14,486	18,228
Great Neck	6,167	7,759	9,654
Great Neck Estates	1,969	2,464	2,809
Great Neck Plaza	2,031	4,246	4,706
Hempstead	20,856	29,135	32,303
Hewlett Bay Park	438	466	519
Hewlett Harbor	228	411	920
Hewlett Neck	163	369	476
Island Park	1,531	2,031	2,318
Kensington	933	978	1,079
Kings Point	1,247	2,445	3,742
Lake Success	203	1,264	2,258
Lattingtown	613	745	886
Laurel Hollow	110	169	248
Lawrence	3,649	4,681	5,609
Lynbrook	14,557	17,314	18,553
Malverne	5,153	8,086	9,386
Manorhaven	484	1,819	2,345
Massapequa Park	487	2,334	8,177

Population of Nassau County and All Units of Government Located Therein in 1940, 1950, and 1954 (cont.)

Unit of Government	1940	1950	1954
Matinecock	428	507	671
Mill Neck	101	505	593
Mineola	10,064	14,831	19,255
Munsey Park	1,456	2,048	2,198
Muttontown	335	382	464
New Hyde Park	4,691	7,349	9,898
North Hills	295	330	337
Old Brookville	356	644	794
Old Westbury	1,017	1,160	1,261
Oyster Bay Cove	466	561	636
Plandome	897	1,102	1,188
Plandome Heights	317	579	598
Plandome Manor	262	323	437
Port Washington North	628	650	650
Rockville Centre	18,613	22,362	25,176
Roslyn	972	1,612	2,383
Roslyn Estates	464	612	895
Roslyn Harbor	303	402	553
Russell Gardens	556	912	1,036
Saddle Rock	69	33	734
Sands Point	628	860	1,220
Sea Cliff	4,416	4,868	5,251
South Floral Park	510	572	673
Stewart Manor	1,625	1,879	2,305
Thomastown	1,159	2,045	2,425
Upper Brookville	456	469	579
Valley Stream	16,679	26,854	32,768
Westbury	4,524	7,112	11,156
Williston Park	5,750	7,505	7,792
Woodsburgh	702	745	911

Sources: Federal Census figures for 1940; Federal Census figures for 1950; Long Island Lighting Company, **Population Survey 1954—Current Population Estimates for Nassau and Suffolk Counties** (Mineola, New York, 1954) [figures are as of January 1, 1954].

Appendix B

Population in Unincorporated Areas
Nassau County

	1950	1954
Kensington North	1,210	1,244
South Saddle Rock	1,315	1,340
Little Neck-South Thomaston	4,179	6,766
Port Washington	12,735	15,882
Manhasset	7,864	9,468
Roslyn Heights	2,871	3,838
Greenvale	1,184	1,626
Albertson	4,729	6,232
Carle Place	3,951	4,719
New Castle	3,179	4,521
Bellerose West	2,283	2,309
Elmont	13,957	21,491
Franklin Square	19,774	25,298
West Hempstead—Lakeview	13,985	18,190
East Hempstead—Uniondale	13,069	17,430
East Meadow	13,881	47,303
Levittown	35,884	52,110
Valley Stream No. and So.	17,168	28,795
Malverne (Uninc.)	3,411	6,046
South Hempstead	4,217	7,560
Roosevelt	8,893	10,584
Oceanside	14,093	21,119
Baldwin	19,521	20,126
Merrick—North Merrick	16,041	21,355
Bellmore—North Bellmore	13,731	18,768
Wantagh	7,096	22,680
Seaford	2,879	9,588
Hewlett	5,629	7,103
Woodmere	7,771	10,328
Inwood	9,842	10,548
Bay Park	1,688	1,875
Island Park (Uninc.)	720	1,835
Atlantic Beach	745	912
Lido—Point Lookout	1,911	2,587
Locust Valley	2,790	3,052
Glenwood Landing	2,185	2,486
Glen Head	2,519	4,195

Population in Unincorporated Areas Nassau County (cont.)

	1950	**1954**
Oyster Bay	5,314	5,777
East Norwich	635	1,858
West Brookville	121	401
Syosset—Cold Spring Area	3,217	5,979
Plainview Area	1,143	8,205
Hicksville	12,070	35,649
Jericho Locust Grove	448	2,953
Bethpage—Plainedge	6,896	21,565
South Farmingdale	1,991	4,843
Massapequa—West Amityville	9,115	20,574

Source: Long Island Lighting Company, **Population Survey 1954—Current Population Estimates for Nassau and Suffolk Counties** (Mineola, New York, 1954).

Appendix C

Area and Data of Incorporated Units of Government in Nassau

Unit of Government	Square Miles	Date of Incorporation
Nassau County	300	1898
Town of Hempstead	24.2	
Town of North Hempstead	53.8	
Town of Oyster Bay	14.6	
City of Glen Cove	6.6	1918
City of Long Beach	2.0	1922
Villages of		
Baxter Estates	0.2	1931
Bayville	1.3	1919
Bellerose	0.1	1924
Brookville	3.2	1931
Cedarhurst	1.1	1910
Centre Island	1.1	1926
Cove Neck	1.5	1927
East Hills	2.2	1931
East Rockaway	1.0	1900
East Williston	0.7	1926
Farmingdale	1.1	1904
Floral Park	1.5	1908
Flower Hill	1.6	1931
Freeport	4.5	1892
Garden City	5.3	1919
Great Neck	1.3	1921
Great Neck Estates	0.8	1911
Great Neck Plaza	0.4	1930
Hempstead	3.7	1853
Hewlett Bay Park	0.5	1928
Hewlett Harbor	0.8	1925
Hewlett Neck	0.2	1927
Island Park	0.4	1926
Kensington	0.2	1921
Kings Point	3.4	1924
Lake Success	1.8	1927
Lattingtown	1.7	1931
Laurel Hollow	0.8	1926
Lawrence	4.5	1897
Lynbrook	2.5	1911
Malverne	1.3	1921
Manorhaven	0.4	1930

Area and Data of Incorporated Units of Government in Nassau (cont.)

Unit of Government	Square Miles	Date of Incorporation
Massapequa Park	1.9	1931
Matinecock	1.3	1928
Mill Neck	2.9	1925
Mineola	1.8	1906
Munsey Park	0.6	1930
Muttontown	3.7	1931
New Hyde Park	1.0	1927
North Hills	3.1	1929
Old Brookville	2.8	1929
Old Westbury	9.0	1924
Oyster Bay Cove	2.6	1931
Plandome	0.5	1911
Plandome Heights	0.1	1929
Plandome Manor	0.5	1931
Port Washington North	0.4	1932
Rockville Centre	2.9	1893
Roslyn	0.6	1932
Roslyn Estates	0.4	1931
Roslyn Harbor	1.1	1931
Russell Gardens	0.1	1931
Saddle Rock	0.4	1911
Sands Point	4.0	1910
Sea Cliff	1.1	1833
South Floral Park	0.2	1925
Stewart Manor	0.2	1927
Thomastown	0.5	1931
Upper Brookville	4.3	1932
Valley Stream	3.6	1925
Williston Park	0.6	1926
Woodsburgh	1.2	1912
Westbury	2.6	1932

Source: New York State, Secretary of State, **Legislative Manual,** 1957, and New York State Department of Audit and Control, **Special Report on Municipal Affairs by the State Comptroller,** 1954.

Appendix D

Total Expenditures[1] for Nassau County and All Units Located Therein Fiscal Years Ending in 1945[2] and 1954[3]

Unit of Government	1945	1954
Nassau County	$15,695,180.56	$ 79,670,780.34
Town of Hempstead	2,115,124.53	12,751,537.88
Town of North Hempstead	1,761,217.59	6,817,659.46
Town of Oyster Bay	683,988.91	6,256,800.07
City of Glen Cove	889,791.53	1,490,310.53
City of Long Beach	2,631,864.17	3,368,349.57
Villages of		
Baxter Estates	2,669.54	21,310.69
Bayville	52,600.77	173,890.06
Bellerose	31,736.72	52,412.38
Brookville	9,564.46	45,477.28
Cedarhurst	217,227.21	338,699.28
Centre Island	20,031.99	43,146.93
Cove Neck	19,728.76	25,993.85
East Hills	16,676.13	94,186.95
East Rockaway	134,263.98	357,426.52
East Williston	41,129.04	101,714.78
Farmingdale	88,315.63	382,707.28
Floral Park	349,957.82	743,307.21
Flower Hill	18,209.26	69,205.11
Freeport	1,157,306.59	4,409,049.47
Garden City	607,835.07	2,503,696.75
Great Neck	180,940.98	453,984.02
Great Neck Estates	119,772.40	241,968.52
Great Neck Plaza	54,961.76	164,926.61
Hempstead	1,313,179.94	3,829,694.91
Hewlett Bay Park	10,362.82	22,645.81
Hewlett Harbor	4,514.72	81,761.50
Hewlett Neck	4,492.25	7,847.28
Island Park	48,786.07	135,132.41
Kensington	39,174.28	124,871.31
Kings Point	100,055.49	268,414.51
Lake Success	62,249.89	186,972.99
Lattingtown	26,908.35	28,638.34
Laurel Hollow	16,887.02	32,034.54
Lawrence	237,515.43	477,429.78
Lynbrook	477,026.30	1,155,340.77
Malverne	170,700.21	527,354.95
Manorhaven	15,360.22	74,125.58
Massapequa Park	29,534.67	277,836.46

Total Expenditures[1] *for Nassau County and All Units Located Therein Fiscal Years Ending in 1945*[2] *and 1954*[3] *(cont.)*

Unit of Government	1945	1954
Matinecock	17,029.18	38,452.67
Mill Neck	26,758.57	47,821.41
Mineola	283,811.68	2,193,208.59
Munsey Park	18,233.60	53,735.79
Muttontown	16,095.42	35,513.56
New Hyde Park	86,699.50	305,953.98
North Hills	3,758.80	10,491.32
Old Brookville	21,911.53	113,399.37
Old Westbury	67,752.64	142,663.20
Oyster Bay Cove	29,566.00	50,731.52
Plandome	56,337.29	113,999.92
Plandome Heights	6,239.88	15,380.89
Plandome Manor	5,078.19	9,811.20
Port Washington North	58.26	12,068.90
Rockville Centre	1,233,878.26	5,330,993.81
Roslyn	32,470.91	101,987.16
Roslyn Estates	12,210.75	23,988.13
Roslyn Harbor	8,693.18	19,386.06
Russell Gardens	11,893.83	53,775.87
Saddle Rock	3,283.97	129,027.52
Sands Point	49,267.72	152,649.66
Sea Cliff	104,649.64	215,082.46
South Floral Park	10,932.38	16,789.05
Stewart Manor	25,086.71	56,191.87
Thomaston	24,192.91	105,939.31
Upper Brookville	15,060.70	45,008.36
Valley Stream	602,987.71	1,727,899.04
Westbury	59,604.13	274,290.56
Williston Park	96,770.51	254,032.26
Woodsburgh	9,818.37	25,782.41
Fire Districts	462,874.47	2,272,415.53
Schools	16,225,552.71	123,059,900.27
TOTAL	$49,085,402.46	$264,817,014.33

[1] Does not include transfers, trust and investment transactions, and refunds.

[2] Figures for 1945 derived from New York State, State Comptroller, **Special Report on Municipal Affairs,** Legislative Document (1946) No. 70 (Albany: Fort Orange Press, 1946).

[3] Figures for 1954 derived from New York State, State Comptroller, **Special Report on Municipal Affairs,** Legislative Document (1955) No. 33A (Albany: Fort Orange Press, 1955) and tabulations made by the New York State Department of Audit and Control, Division of Municipal Affairs, Research and Statistics Section, November, 1955, from annual reports filed in the comptroller's office.

Appendix E

The State Constitution provides[1] for the following limitations on local indebtedness which are based on a percentage of the average full valuation, over the preceding five years, of the taxable real estate of the jurisdiction involved:

The County of Nassau, for county purposes, ten per cent.

Any town, for town purposes, seven per cent.

Any city having less than one hundred twenty-five thousand inhabitants, for city purposes, excluding education purposes, seven per cent.

The Constitutional limitations[2] on the amount to be raised by real estate taxes for current expenses for local government purposes are also based on a percentage of the average full valuation of the taxable real estate:

Any county, for county purposes, one and one-half per cent (this limitation can be increased to two per cent).

Any city of less than one hundred twenty-five thousand inhabitants, for city purposes, excluding education, two per cent.

Any village, for village purposes, two per cent.

There are no limitations for town purposes or school district purposes except when the school district lies partly within a city of less than 125,000 people.

[1] New York State Constitution, Article VIII, Section 4.
[2] New York State Constitution, Article VIII, Section 10.

Appendix F

Percentage Distribution of Income by Source for Nassau County and All Units Located Therein for Fiscal Years Ending in 1954

B. = Borrowing; R. = Revenue

Source	Total	County	Cities	Towns	Villages	School Dists.	Fire Dists.
Borrowing and Revenue	100.00	100.00	100.00	100.00	100.00	100.00	100.00
Per Cent of B. R. Borrowing	34.79	26.46	12.24	29.40	31.43	41.85	3.58
Per Cent of B. R. Revenue	65.21	73.54	87.76	70.60	68.57	58.15	96.42
Revenue	100.00	100.00	100.00	100.00	100.00	100.00	100.00
Per Cent of R. Assessments	10.55	17.16		39.60	3.95		77.16
Per Cent of R. Local Non-Property Taxes	1.57	5.03	3.56			.07	
Per Cent of R. State Aid	18.44	11.00	7.25	20.01	8.81	26.07	
Per Cent of R. Real Estate Tax	54.08	53.31	56.50	20.56	57.59	62.68	
Per Cent of R. Federal Aid	2.25	3.19	.02	.006		2.85	
Per Cent of R. Other	13.08	10.31	32.67	19.82	29.64	8.30	22.84

Source: Table 29, p. 84.

Appendix G

Income[1] *by Source for Nassau County and All Units Located Therein—Fiscal Years Ending in 1945*

Source	Total	County	Cities	Towns	Villages	School Districts	Fire Districts
Borrowing and Revenue	$50,599,233.20	$16,495,486.09	$3,808,322.42	$4,597,818.55	$9,002,770.90	$16,193,758.74	$500,716.50
Borrowings	1,636,103.08	50,000.00	302,651.08	163,069.29	1,097,397.26	—[2]	22,985.45
Revenue	48,963,130.12	16,445,846.09	3,505,671,34	4,434,749.26	7,905,373.64	16,193,758.74	477,731.05
Assessments	$ 2,136,384.33		$ 219,392.89	$1,815,388.11	$ 101,603.33		
State Aid & Federal Aid	5,652,752.51	$ 1,392,073.92	214,984.50	59,785.62	20,856.80	$ 3,965,051.67	
Shared Tax	2,547,260.13	719,192.26	106,120.05	868,896.88	853,050.94		
Mortgage Tax	224,455.58		11,746.87	185,420.32	27,288.39		
Real Estate Tax	32,905,071.02	12,698,443.60	2,155,613.36	866,253.39	4,968,383.21	11,772,383.11	$443,994.35
Other	5,481,273.56	1,636,136.31	781,880.68	639,004.94	1,934,190.97	456,323.96	33,736.70
Local Non-Property Taxes	15,932.99		15,932.99				

[1] Does not include transfers, trust and investment transactions, or the balance at the beginning of the year.

[2] This figure not available. Judging by the 1945–1946 figures, it would probably be about 10 per cent of the revenue figure.

Source: Figures derived from New York State, State Comptroller, **Special Report on Municipal Affairs,** Legislative Document (1946) No. 70 (Albany Fort Orange Press, 1946).

Appendix H

School District Tax Rate

	1945	1950	1954
Town of Hempstead			
Uniondale	$ .95	$1.84	$2.86
East Meadow	1.18	2.05	2.92
North Bellmore	1.17	2.18	3.85
Jerusalem	.28	1.80	3.67
Seaford	1.15	2.49	3.52
Bellmore	1.41	2.03	4.31
Roosevelt	1.41	2.08	2.76
Freeport	1.35	1.95	2.87
Baldwin	1.20	1.88	3.24
Oceanside	1.15	1.66	3.50
No. Lynbrook & Malverne	1.37	1.81	2.73
Valley Stream	1.46	1.91	3.67
Woodmere-Hewlett	1.215	2.185	3.767
Lawrence	1.39	1.86	2.984
Elmont	1.57	2.102	3.30
Franklin Square	1.55	2.42	3.61
Garden City	1.15	1.71	2.32
East Rockaway	1.39	1.72	2.93
Lynbrook	1.34	1.83	3.30
Rockville Centre	1.09	1.69	2.98
Floral Park	1.24	1.70	2.82
Wantagh	1.16	2.56	4.45
Valley Stream	1.37	1.90	3.65
Merrick	1.33	1.66	4.27
Island Trees	.64	1.87	3.46
West Hempstead	1.38	1.945	3.53
Long Beach	1.3587	1.967	2.629
North Merrick	1.63	2.49	4.17
Valley Stream	1.40	2.44	3.40
Island Park	1.30	1.47	2.42
Central High School		Included in School Districts	
Sewanhaka High School		Included in School Districts	
Mepham High School		Included in School Districts	
Town of North Hempstead			
Westbury	1.321	1.934	2.71
East Williston	.63	1.77	2.98
Roslyn	1.596	2.423	3.51
Port Washington	1.16	1.94	2.93
New Hyde Park	1.23	2.075	2.953

School District Tax Rate (cont.)

	1945	1950	1954
Manhasset	1.322	1.99	2.991
Great Neck	1.14	2.24	3.53
Jericho—Williston Park	1.34	2.17	3.89
Mineola	1.21	2.10	2.92
Carle Place	1.24	2.06	3.05
Glenwood Landing	.551	1.31	1.85
Glen Head	.755	1.334	1.96
Brookville	.325	.605	1.11
Locust Valley	.68	1.07	1.56
Glen Cove (included with City)			
Bayville	.97	1.32	2.19
Sanatorium		County Property	
East Norwich	.37	.6993	1.366
Oyster Bay	.76	1.35	1.54
Cold Spring Harbor	.527	.96	2.104
Syosset	.78	.96	2.474
Woodbury	.435	.65	2.594
Locust Grove	.79	1.23	2.47
Jericho-Wheatley	.3916	.622	1.15
Hicksville	1.44	2.13	3.56
Plainedge—Central Park	.61	2.36	3.39
Plainview	.62	1.93	2.77
Bethpage—Old	.84	1.13	2.36
Bethpage	1.00	1.63	3.00
Farmingdale	.89	1.03	2.56
Massapequa	.85	2.16	3.49
Sea Cliff	1.42	1.78	1.76
Amityville (Nassau portion)	.89	1.67	3.393

Source: Five-Year Cumulative Report of County of Nassau, New York, and all Municipal Subdivisions as of December 31, 1945 and December 31, 1954. This annual report is prepared by the county comptroller, Mineola, New York.

Appendix I

Village Rates

Unit of Government	1945	1950	1954
Villages of			
Baxter Estates	$ .05	$ .08	$ .15
Bayville	.72	1.05	1.35
Bellerose	.75	.95	1.10
Brookville	.20	.22	.32
Cedarhurst	1.10	1.30	1.30
Centre Island	.75	.98	1.22
Cove Neck	.60	.76	.76
East Hills	.40	.65	.575
East Rockaway	.90	1.00	1.25
East Williston	.789	.95	1.22
Farmingdale	.73	1.00	1.30
Floral Park	1.01	1.42	1.68
Flower Hill	.30	.45	.45
Freeport	1.33	1.52	1.75
Garden City	.87	1.34	1.68
Great Neck	.95	1.16	1.33
Great Neck Estates	.95	1.25	1.57
Great Neck Plaza	.76	.95	1.00
Hempstead	1.34	1.82	2.00
Hewlett Bay Park	.40	.55	.55
Hewlett Harbor	.14	.25	.45
Hewlett Neck	.16	.20	.20
Island Park	1.50	2.10	2.05
Kensington	.89	1.25	1.60
Kings Point	.52	.86	1.06
Lake Success	.399	.56	.865
Lattingtown	.32	.09	.12
Laurel Hollow	1.11	1.01	1.38
Lawrence	1.00	1.00	.94
Lynbrook	1.02	1.42	1.56
Malverne	.86	1.49	2.14
Manorhaven	.60	.70	.80
Massapequa Park	1.74	1.38	1.24
Matinecock	.21	.44	.50
Mill Neck	.37	.61	.606
Mineola	1.00	1.04	1.40
Munsey Park	.20	.70	.77
Muttontown	.17	.50	.50
New Hyde Park	.88	1.00	1.15

Village Rates (cont.)

Unit of Government	1945	1950	1954
North Hills	.12	.10	.10
Old Brookville	.21	.40	.50
Old Westbury	.15	.36	.52
Oyster Bay Cove	.41	.582	.58
Plandome	.89	1.15	1.48
Plandome Heights	.28	.29	.33
Plandome Manor	.11	.18	.16
Port Washington North	None	None	.60
Rockville Centre	.99	1.48	1.65
Roslyn	.90	.90	.96
Roslyn Estates	.42	.54	.54
Roslyn Harbor	.38	.55	.50
Russell Gardens	.35	.50	.575
Saddle Rock	.133	1.05	1.34
Sands Point	.20	.49	.49
Sea Cliff	1.46	1.34	1.60
South Floral Park	1.70	1.60	1.60
Stewart Manor	.75	1.07	1.15
Thomaston	.43	1.47	1.87
Upper Brookville	.20	.40	.65
Valley Stream	1.06	1.38	1.42
Westbury	.80	1.20	1.33
Williston Park	.56	1.04	1.10
Woodsburgh	.18	.32	.35

Source: Five-Year Cumulative Report of County of Nassau, New York, and all Municipal Subdivisions, issued in 1950 and 1954 by the county comptroller, Mineola, New York.

Appendix J

Estimated Revenue and Unexpended Balance of the Town of Hempstead, 1954

Estimated Revenue		
Per Capita Assistance, Etc.	$1,138,078.00	
Administration Charges	26,750.00	
Court Fines	4,000.00	
Dog License Fees	47,000.00	
Dumping Fees	6,500.00	
Mortgage Tax	600,000.00	
Road Opening Permits	8,000.00	
Rent—Town Owned Property	20,000.00	
Animal Shelter	6,500.00	
Board Zoning Appeals	8,000.00	
Building Department Fees	110,000.00	
Engineering Department Fees	7,500.00	
Department of Parks Fees	75,000.00	
Registrar's Fees	4,000.00	
Town Attorney's Fees	1,500.00	
Town Clerk's Fees	35,000.00	
Rock Hall Memorial Fees	2,000.00	$2,099,828.00
Estimated Unexpended Balance December 31, 1953		
Animal Shelter	$ 10,000.00	
Board of Zoning Appeals	10,000.00	
Building Department	20,000.00	
Engineering Department	25,000.00	
Photostat Department	5,000.00	
Receiver of Taxes	30,000.00	
Supervisor	10,000.00	
Town Attorney	8,000.00	
Town Clerk	15,000.00	
Town Comptroller	5,000.00	
Town Hall	20,000.00	
Compensation Insurance	5,000.00	
Waterways and Public Lands	50,000.00	
Employees Retirement	13,000.00	
Town Historian	500.00	
Surplus	834,942.17	$1,061,442.17
		$3,161,270.17

Source: Annual Budget of Revenue and Expenditures of the Town of Hempstead for the fiscal year 1954.